CLASSICAL QUILLS II

TEACHER'S EDITION

EILEEN CUNNINGHAM

Edited by Amy Alexander Carmichael

Lochinvar Press
Wichita, KS

Text Copyright © 2015 Eileen Cunningham and Amy Alexander Carmichael

ISBN: 978-0692514047

All rights reserved.

To the community of the

Classical School of Wichita

Wichita, Kansas

Table of Contents

CHAPTER 1: FABLE 1

CHAPTER 2: DESCRIPTION 11

CHAPTER 3: NARRATIVE 29

CHAPTER 4: WRITING A GOOD PARAGRAPH 49

CHAPTER 5: PROVERB AND CHREIA 63

CHAPTER 6: ENCOMIUM AND INVECTIVE 81

CHAPTER 7: REFUTATION AND CONFIRMATION 93

CHAPTER 8: COMMONPLACE 117

CHAPTER 9: COMPARISON 129

CHAPTER 10: SPEECH-IN-CHARACTER 141

CHAPTER 11: THESIS 157

CHAPTER 12: LAW 171

INTRODUCTION

Definition of *Progymnasmata*

The Greek word *progymnasmata* (pro-goom-NAHZ-ma-tuh) is composed of the prefix *pro-* (*fore, pre-*) and the root *–gymnas* (*exercise*). Together, they are rendered in English as the early or preliminary exercises. To be specific, they are the exercises rhetoric teachers considered foundational to the study of rhetoric. A student was expected to have mastered them before beginning actual rhetoric classes.

History of the Progymnasmata

The earliest mention of the progymnasmata can be found in a rhetorical handbook dated to the fourth century BC. By the first century AD, separate handbooks for the progymnasmata were written and circulated. Perhaps the most famous handbooks were written by Hermogenes of Tarsus in the second century AD and the great orator Aphthonius in the fourth century AD.[1]

Aphthonius included fourteen exercises in his handbook:

Fable (*Mythos*)	Commonplace (*Koinos topos*)
Narrative (*Diêgêma*)	Encomium (*Enkōmion*)
Description (*Ekphrasis*)	Invective (*Psogos*)
Proverb (*Gnōmê*)	Comparison (*Synkrisis*)
Anecdote (*Chreia*)	Speech in Character (*Prosōpopoeia*)

Refutation (*Anaskeuê*)   Thesis (*Thesis*)
Confirmation (*Kataskeuê*)   Legislation (*Nomos*)

In our earlier books, *Writing the Classical Way I* and *II*, we included all fourteen of the elements and introduced all approaches for each. But when it was decided to introduce classical composition to students in the last two years of grammar school (fifth and sixth grades), we combined similar elements of the progymnasmata together and reduced the number of approaches, fitting *Classical Quills I* and *II* more suitably to the age group. Thus, Proverb and Chreia appear together as do Refutation/Confirmation, and Encomium/Invective. *Classical Quills I* was further abridged by omitting the last two elements, Thesis and Law.

A chapter entitled "Writing a Good Paragraph" has also been included so that students can learn to present material deductively, moving from general to specific, which is the foundational pattern of discourse among the English-speaking peoples.

Values-Based Education

The ideal of a Greek education was to produce "a good man speaking well." First the progymnasmata and then the study of rhetoric certainly assist the student to speak (or write) well, but the first part of the motto must not be forgotten: classical education is equally concerned with teaching students to think morally and ethically. This focus may be one of the main reasons why the Judeo-Christian world was able to adopt Greco-Roman education so readily: it cultivated virtue.

Nowhere is this emphasis more clear than in the progymnasmata itself. Every one of the elements—from Fable to Law—asks students to address issues of morality and, in a Christian context, to hold everything up to the standards of moral and ethical conduct set out in Scripture.

This feature of education, designed by pagan Greeks and Romans, has been nearly abandoned in many public schools in the United States today, but the desire of many to re-institute what we now call *values-based education* finds satisfaction in the routine elements of the progymnasmata. For this reason, if for no other, Christian schools should introduce the progymnasmata to children at the earliest possible stage so that they can begin to craft their responses to the issues facing our culture in ways compatible with their faith.

Teacher's Edition

Grammar, Logic, and Rhetoric Stages in *Classical Quills*

Each chapter begins with definitions and examples. These constitute the Grammar Stage.

Definitions and examples are followed by "Think It Through" questions, where students apply the concepts to their own experience. Model compositions come next, followed by student analysis of the model. These constitute the Logic stage.

Finally, students are asked to explore ways to use the element to address issues within their own experience. The chapter ends with an original composition on a debatable issue. These constitute the Rhetoric stage.

A Note on Readiness

In his text *Institutes of Oratory*, Quintilian, a Roman rhetorician of the first century AD, addressed the issue of age-appropriateness, saying: "I think that the question when a boy ought to be sent to the teacher of rhetoric is best decided by the answer, when he shall be qualified."[2] Today chronological age governs school progress more than mental readiness, yet teachers still must make decisions everyday as to whether students are ready for X or Y. Therefore, within the context of the individual classroom, the teacher may find that there are some students who are not ready to engage the later elements—such as Refutation/Confirmation, Thesis, and Law. This is not a failure of the teacher or the student. This is simply the nature of growth. For this reason, the classroom teacher or homeschooling parent is encouraged to use discretion.

The models in these later chapters have been selected with a nod toward chronological age. Models for both volumes are pulled from great works of children's literature such as *Alice in Wonderland, Oliver Twist, The Adventures of Huckleberry Finn,* and *Peter Pan.* Issues for discussion and debate are related to the life experience of the age group—defending a classmate wrongly accused of cheating (Refutation), providing reasons for and against offering classes in Spanish (Thesis), arguing for or against requiring the licensure of bicyclists (Law). It is believed students will naturally have strong feelings about such issues, and what remains is for the teacher to give the students the tools they need to help them articulate their ideas in a clear-headed manner.

We are well advised to use common sense in order to present the progymnasmata in a way that challenges but does not frustrate students. For those more difficult exercises in the later chapters, perhaps guided writing, using laptop projectors or—what students sometimes prefer—a class "scribe" at the board, should supersede the assignment of individual compositions written alone as homework. Students who are ready to fly solo, so to speak, should also be encouraged to do so. It is the teacher's call.

The production of a Scope and Sequence within the context of the individual school would also provide teachers with some guidance in these matters.

Scripture References in *Classical Quills*

Unless otherwise specified, the English Standard Version of the Bible has been used throughout *Classical Quills* I and II.

Acknowledgements

We wish to thank the Classical School of Wichita's board, administration, faculty, parents, and students for supporting us in this project. Special thanks to teachers Kris Darrah and Michelle Young and to student Hannah M. for testing the materials. Their feedback has encouraged us and improved the materials greatly. Any errors that might remain are, of course, our own. We are committed to producing materials of a quality which honors our Lord and Savior, Jesus Christ: "Whatever you do, work heartily, as for the Lord and not for men, knowing that from the Lord you will receive the inheritance as your reward. You are serving the Lord Christ" (Col. 3:23–24). In order to improve the work to achieve the highest standard, we welcome input from all who use or have an interest in these materials.

Contact Information

Please feel free to contact us with questions, observations, or suggestions at LochinvarPress@cox.net.

FABLE

Chapter 1

Introduction

Once, when a Lion was asleep, a little Mouse began running up and down upon him. This soon wakened the Lion, who placed his huge paw upon him, and opened his big jaws to swallow him. "Pardon, O King," cried the little Mouse, "forgive me this time, I shall never forget it! I may be able to return the favor one of these day?" The Lion was so tickled at the idea of the Mouse being able to help him that he lifted up his paw and let him go.  Some time after, the Lion was caught in a trap, and the hunters, who desired to carry him alive to the King, tied him to a tree while they went in search of a wagon to carry him on. Just then the little Mouse happened to pass by, and seeing the sad plight of the Lion, went up to him and soon gnawed away the ropes that bound the King of the Beasts. "Was I not right?" said the little Mouse.

Moral: Little friends may prove great friends.[3]

Tales like "The Lion and the Mouse" are what we call *fables*. The most famous fable writer ever was probably Aesop, who dwelt in ancient Greece. In ancient Greece and Rome, parents and teachers would use fables to teach children truths about life. For example, "The

Lion and the Mouse" shows that little people (perhaps "ordinary folk") are just as important as big people (perhaps the rulers of the country).

However, the ancients did not use fables just for the instruction of children. They often applied them to the great events of history. Look at the fable "The Wolf and the Crane," for example:

The Wolf and the Crane
By Aesop

A Wolf had been gorging on an animal he had killed, when suddenly a small bone in the meat stuck in his throat and he could not swallow it. He soon felt terrible pain in his throat, and ran up and down groaning and groaning and seeking for something to relieve the pain. He tried to induce every one he met to remove the bone. "I would give anything," said he, "if you would take it out." At last the Crane agreed to try, and told the Wolf to lie on his side and open his jaws as wide as he could. Then the Crane put its long neck down the Wolf's throat, and with its beak loosened the bone, till at last it got it out.

"Will you kindly give me the reward you promised?" said the Crane.

The Wolf grinned and showed his teeth and said: "Be content. You have put your head inside a Wolf's mouth and taken it out again in safety; that ought to be reward enough for you."

Moral: Gratitude and greed go not together.[4]

During the reign of the Roman emperor Hadrian (AD 117-138), this fable was used by the Jewish sage Joshua ben Hananiah. His hope was that the Jewish people would not rebel against Rome. Doing so, he thought, would be similar to putting their heads into the jaws of the lion.

Hananiah's use of the fable illustrates another aspect of fables: They can be found in all cultures and in all time periods—sometimes unique to a culture and sometimes borrowed from a different culture. Certainly the Jewish writers of the Old Testament used fables, and in the New Testament, we also see the parables of Jesus.

Teacher's Edition

Definition and Purpose of a Fable

A fable is a very short story that can be used in one of these ways:

1. Parents and teachers can use fables to teach children proper behavior.
2. Leaders can use fables to persuade others to a certain course of action.
3. Religious leaders can use fables—more commonly called *parables* in the New Testament—to teach spiritual lessons.

 **THINK IT THROUGH:** Read the following parables of Jesus together as a class. What spiritual lessons do the parables make?

- "The Mustard Seed" (Mark 4:30-32)
  Answers will vary, but one possible interpretation is that the kingdom of God grows even from the work of one or a few believers.
- "Signs from a Fig Tree" (Matthew 24:32-35)
  Answers will vary, but Jesus has just been talking about the coming of the Son of Man, so he was probably telling his disciples that the time of redemption was near. Perhaps he meant that at the end of the world there will be signs.

Characteristics of the Fable

1. **Characters:** The characters in a fable can be people, animals, or even things (such as trees or rivers). In some fables, there might be a mixture of two or more character types.

   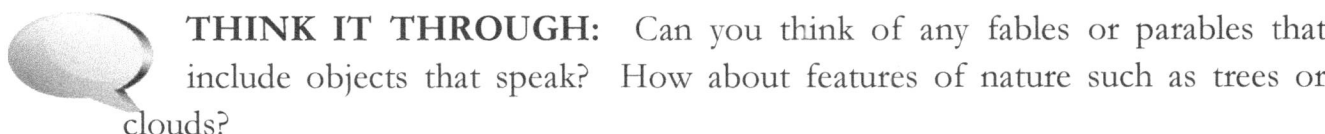 **THINK IT THROUGH:** Can you think of any fables or parables that include objects that speak? How about features of nature such as trees or clouds?

2. **Names:** The characters normally do not have names such as "Marcus" or "Pharos." Rather, as we see above, they are just called "Crane" or "Wolf."

    **THINK IT THROUGH:** Look again at the fables that appear above and notice the use of capitalization. Why do you think writers of fables often capitalize these common nouns (such as *Crane* and *Wolf*)?

3. **Moral:** The fable should end with a moral to be learned. It normally appears at the end of the fable.

 # EXERCISE 1.1: Analyzing Fables and Parables

<u>Directions</u>: Please read the fables below and answer the questions that follow.

The Serpent and the Eagle
By Aesop

A Serpent and an Eagle were struggling with each other in deadly conflict. The Serpent had the advantage and was about to strangle the bird. A countryman saw them, and running up, loosed the coil of the Serpent and let the Eagle go free. The Serpent, irritated at the escape of his prey, injected his poison into the drinking horn of the countryman. The rustic, ignorant of his danger, was about to drink, when the Eagle struck his hand with his wing, and, seizing the drinking horn in his talons, carried it aloft.

Moral: One good turn deserves another.[5]

Questions:

1. Re-tell the story in one or two sentences.

   A man saved an eagle from the serpent, and then the eagle saved the man from the serpent.

2. What kind of characters appear in this fable: humans, animals, objects, or a mixture?

   The fable has a mixture of characters: human and animal.

3. What is the moral to the fable?

   One good turn deserves another.

Teacher's Edition

4. Where is the moral located?

   The moral is located at the end of the fable.

The Parable of the Persistent Widow
Luke 18:1-8

And he [Jesus] told them a parable to the effect that they ought always to pray and not lose heart. ² He said, "In a certain city there was a judge who neither feared God nor respected man. ³ And there was a widow in that city who kept coming to him and saying, 'Give me justice against my adversary.' ⁴ For a while he refused, but afterward he said to himself, 'Though I neither fear God nor respect man, ⁵ yet because this widow keeps bothering me, I will give her justice, so that she will not beat me down by her continual coming.'" ⁶ And the Lord said, "Hear what the unrighteous judge says. ⁷ And will not God give justice to his elect, who cry to him day and night? Will he delay long over them? ⁸ I tell you, he will give justice to them speedily. Nevertheless, when the Son of Man comes, will he find faith on earth?"

Questions:

1. What kind of characters are in this parable: human, animal, objects, or a mixture?

   The characters are humans.

2. In which verses is the point of the parable (the moral) explained?

   The moral is explained in verses 6-8.

3. In your own words, briefly state the lesson (moral) of the parable.

   Answers will vary, but one possibility is that the Lord will provide justice speedily to those who cry out to Him.

The Expanded Fable

Sometimes writers will take a familiar fable of just three or four sentences and expand it into a longer story. To do this, they add dialogue and descriptive detail not found in the original. In fact, sometimes filmmakers will even create a movie out of a fable or parable.

Word Choice in an Expanded Fable

The words of a fable are normally quite simple. However, when converting a short fable into an expanded version, a writer should follow the fundamental skill of a storyteller: "Show, don't tell!" This means that a good writer chooses precise words rather than vague words in order to give the story an authentic air.

For example, the original fable might read as follows:

"Some time after, the Lion was caught in a trap."

But students who expand the fable would want to do more than just report what happened in such a simple way. They might want to make the story a bit more colorful, thus:

A few days later, when the Lion had nearly forgotten the incident, he was strolling peacefully through the jungle, enjoying the little spots of sunlight that flickered here and there on the jungle floor beneath the many branches of the trees. Suddenly, "Swish! Clank!" He was caught in a trap, and there seemed no one about to help him. "Yikes! I'm in a fix now!" he lamented.

EXERCISE 1.2: Examining an Expanded Fable

<u>Directions</u>: To examine various techniques for expanding a fable, please answer the questions below.

1. What verb was chosen to say that the lion was *walking* through the jungle?

   Strolling

2. What details were added to show what the lion was seeing?

   Details about the play of light through the leaves on the trees

3. In the expanded version, instead of simply saying the Lion was "caught in a trap," what did the author add to spice it up a bit?

   The sounds "Swish! Clank!"

4. What dialogue was added to show the Lion's reaction?

   "Yikes! I'm in a fix now."

5. What word has the writer chosen to avoid the over-used word *said*?

   lamented

Model Expanded Fable

The Boy and the Filberts
By Aesop

Original Version

A Boy put his hand into a pitcher full of filberts. He grasped as many as he could possibly hold, but when he tried to pull out his hand, he was prevented from doing so by the neck of the pitcher. Unwilling to lose his filberts, and yet unable to withdraw his hand, he burst into tears and bitterly lamented his disappointment. A bystander said to him, "Be satisfied with half the quantity, and you will readily draw out your hand."

Moral: Do not attempt too much at once.[6]

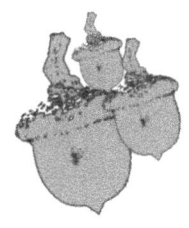

Expanded Version

One day a Boy had a long wait between lunch and dinner. Hungry for a snack, he eyed a pitcher full of filberts which someone had placed on a table. "Filberts!" he blurted. "My favorite!" His mouth began to water as he imagined himself savoring each of the luscious filberts in the pitcher. With nary a thought of the consequences, he plunged his hand into the pitcher and filled his hand with as many of the nuts as he could possibly hold. His plan was to filch the filberts, eat a few, and hide the rest under his pillow in the manner of a squirrel stockpiling acorns for the winter. "Yum!" he thought as his mouth began to water. He squeezed his hand inside the jar, grabbed a fistful of filberts, and started to withdraw his hand, anxious to crack one open and savor it. But quickly he discovered that the mouth of the pitcher was too narrow, and his hand was perfectly stuck. He tugged. He pulled. He twisted. He tightened his fingers till his fingernails dug into his flesh, trying to make his fist just a wee bit smaller. But, alas! Nothing would work. "Wah!" he howled, bursting into tears. No matter what he did, his hand with all the luscious filberts could not pass through the opening. About that time, a passerby, seeing the Boy's predicament, stopped and watched the struggle between the fist and the pitcher. "Ohh! Ugh!" the Boy grunted. "I say, my friend," began the passerby. "May I make a suggestion?" The Boy could barely respond, so intent was he on pulling out his hand. "Why don't you let a few of those filberts fall back into the pitcher? Then your hand will be smaller, and you'll be able to draw it out with ease." At his wit's end by now, the Boy took the bystander's advice. Plunk! Plunk! Plunk! He dropped a few filberts back into the pitcher, and—hooray!—just as the bystander had said, the Boy was able to withdraw his hand quite speedily. "Thank you, kind sir!" he exclaimed as he ran off with his few tasty filberts.

Moral: Do not attempt too much at once.

EXERCISE 1.3: Analyzing an Expanded Fable

Directions: Analyze the expanded version "The Boy and the Filberts" by answering the questions below.

1. In your own words, summarize the fable of "The Boy and the Filberts."

    A boy puts his hand into a pitcher in order to pull out some filberts. However, he takes so many that he cannot pull his hand out of the pitcher. A passerby tells him to drop a few filberts back into the pitcher, and then he is able to remove his hand.

Teacher's Edition

2. What is the moral of "The Boy and the Filberts"?

   Do not attempt too much at once.

3. With a highlighter, highlight all the dialogue that was added in the expanded version of the fable, including both speech and thoughts.

4. When writing the conversation between the Boy and the passerby, the writer has selected verbs that can be used to introduce the characters' words. If the writer used the tags *the boy said* and *the bystander said* in every case, the fable would be a bit weak. In the space provided, write down all the stronger verbs that the writer used in place of *say*? The first one serves as an example.

   a. "Filberts!" he *blurted*   .

   b. "Yum!" he *thought*   as his mouth began to water.

   c. "Wah!" he *howled*   .

   d. "I say, my friend," *began*   the passerby.

   e. "Thank you, kind sir!" he *exclaimed*   .

EXERCISE 1.4: Expanding a Fable with a Partner

Directions: Read the following Fable. Then with a partner expand it by adding dialogue and details. Avoid using ordinary verbs like *said* and *asked*. Be prepared to read your work orally to the class.

The Lion and the Three Bulls
By Aesop

Three Bulls for a long time pastured together. A Lion lay in ambush in the hope of making them his prey, but was afraid to attack them while they kept together. Having at last by guileful speeches succeeded in separating them, he attacked them without fear as they fed alone, and feasted on them one by one at his own leisure.

Moral: Union is strength.[7]

Quills #1: Expanding a Fable

The teacher will give you a simple fable. Your task will be to write an Expanded Fable by adding dialogue and colorful details. Remember to use colorful verbs.

Quills #2: Writing a Fable

The teacher will give you a list of "morals to the story." Your task will be to create a Fable that teaches the moral.

DESCRIPTION

Chapter 2

Introduction

What is it to describe a person? Take Abraham Lincoln, for example. Probably no other public figure has been called "ugly" as many times as he was—mostly before and during his presidency. Yet, people who appreciate his great spirit have more often described his character than his looks. The difference can be seen in the paragraphs below. The first was written in 1862 by a London journalist describing Lincoln's physical appearance for his readers back in England:

> To say that he is ugly is nothing; to add that his figure is grotesque, is to convey no adequate impression. Fancy a man 6 feet high and thin out of proportion; with long bony arms and legs which somehow seem to be always in the way with great rugged furrowed hands which grab you like a vice when shaking yours; with a long scraggy neck and a chest too narrow for the great arms at his side. Add to this figure a head, coconut shaped and somewhat too small for such a stature, covered with rough uncombed and uncombable hair, that stands out in every direction at once. . . .[8]

Now look at a description of Lincoln's personality, written by Frederick Douglass, an educated former slave active in the abolitionist movement:

I have been down there to see the President; and as you were not there, perhaps you would like to know how the President of the United States received a black man at the White House. I will tell you how he received me—just as you see one gentleman receive another; with a hand and a voice, well balanced between a kind cordiality and a respectful reserve. I tell you I felt big there.[9]

From these two examples, one sees that there are different approaches to description. You will have the chance to practice some of them in this chapter.

Methods of Describing People

In classical times, the composition teachers identified six methods that are used when describing people:

- Name
- Age
- Gender (male or female)
- Nationality (or ethnic group)
- Appearance
- Mental state
- Emotional State

> To help memorize these methods, you can turn them into an acronym by using the first letter of each word: NAGNAME.

Now, the term *Appearance* is a very broad term. Following is a list of subdivisions that will assist you in writing a complete description:

- Appearance
    - Physical Characteristics
        - Body form
        - Facial expression
        - Voice

- Posture
- Physical abilities
- Physical disabilities (infirmities)
  - Clothing
  - Manner

NOTE: It is important to remember that people are unique. Therefore, writers pick and choose which of the approaches they will use to describe the particular person who is their topic. For example, if a person has no disabilities, the writer simply skips that topic.

THINK IT THROUGH: With your classmates, read this description about Julius Caesar, which is based on a description by the Roman writer Suetonius (AD 70-130). Then, as a class, look for the various methods Suetonius used in this description by answering the questions that follow.

Julius Caesar (100 BC – 44 BC) was tall and light-skinned. His arms and legs were round, and he had a rather full face with black, piercing eyes. He had excellent health except that near the end of his life he had sudden fainting fits and did not sleep well. Twice in his life he was seized with the "falling sickness" (epilepsy) while in active service. He was extremely fussy in personal grooming. He kept the hair of his head closely cut and his face smoothly shaved. He was greatly bothered by his baldness, especially after he found himself the object of the jibes of his enemies. Therefore, he used to brush his hair forward from the crown of his head, and was greatly pleased that the Senate and People conferred honors on him that allowed him constantly to wear a laurel crown [see image]. It is said that he was particular in his dress, for he wore the *latus clavus* with fringes about the wrists.[10]

Name: What is the name of the person whom Suetonius is describing? *Julius Caesar*

Age: Suetonius does not directly state an age, but he does describe an older man and talk about his health near the time of his death. Using the dates in the first sentence, figure out how old Caesar was at the time of his assassination in 44 BC. *about 56*

Gender: Obviously Julius Caesar was a man, but what characteristic of older men seems to have afflicted Caesar? *Baldness*

Nationality: Though this paragraph does not directly state Caesar's nationality, indicate his nationality in the space provided.

Caesar was a Roman.

Appearance:

- **Physical characteristics**
    - Was Caesar tall or short? *Tall*
    - Was his skin dark or light toned? *Light*
    - What was his bodily form? *Rounded arms and legs*
    - What color were his eyes? *Black*
    - Did he have short or long hair? *Short*
    - Was he shaven or bearded? *Shaven*
    - Did he have any infirmities (ailments)? *Fainting fits, insomnia, epilepsy*
    - How did he comb his hair? *Combed forward from the crown*

- **Clothing**
    - What did he often wear on his head? *A laurel crown*
    - What decorative feature of clothing did he have around his wrists when he wore the *latus clavus* (a toga with a purple stripe)? *Fringe*

- **Manner**
    - He was *fussy* about personal grooming.
    - He was *particular* in his dress.

- **Mental/Emotional State:** From the details about Caesar's hair and clothing, what can we assume about Caesar's personality? *He was a bit vain.*

EXERCISE 2.1: Examining a Description of a Person

Directions: Please begin by reading the introductory note about the athlete Jim Thorpe. Next, read the excerpt from a 1922 newspaper article in which Thorpe is described. Then complete the chart which follows.

Jim Thorpe 1910

Note: James Francis "Jim" Thorpe (1888-1953) was an American athlete of Native American and European ancestry. A member of the Sac and Fox tribe, Jim was originally named Wa-Tho-Huk, which means "Bright Path." He is still considered one of the greatest athletes of all time. He won gold medals at the Olympics in 1912 in the decathlon and pentathlon. He also played football, basketball, and baseball. Athletes participating in the Olympics at that time were required to be amateur athletes. An athlete who played professionally in any sport was not eligible to participate in the Olympics. Unfortunately, Thorpe had played professional baseball in 1909 and 1910, so when this was revealed in 1913, he was stripped of his Olympic gold medals. Subsequently, he played professionally in football, baseball, and basketball.

Excerpt from "Indian Thorpe Greatest Sport Marvel of All Time"
By Robert Edgren

Jim Thorpe is now thirty-seven years old and plays for the Cleveland Tigers [football team]. He plans to play one more season and then retire to ranching. . . .

Thorpe was the most sensational football player in the country when on the Carlisle [Indian] team. Six feet tall, powerfully but lightly built and weighing about 180 pounds, Thorpe combined speed and a quick brain with great aggressiveness and a natural knack of handling himself and the ball. He was versatile. As a drop kicker and a placement kicker, he had no equal. In one game against an Eastern college, he kicked four field goals in four attempts.

Playing against West Point, Thorpe scored all the Carlisle points himself, making touchdowns, field goals, goal kicks and scoring by every means known except by a "safety." He was a strong and fast runner, and is still.

When Thorpe had won all possible football honors, he gave part of his time to other sports. As a track athlete he put over a number of very fine performances. Going to Sweden to the Olympic Games of 1912, he won the Decathlon, 800 points ahead of his nearest competitor, H. Weislander of Sweden. It was after these games Thorpe was declared a professional because he had played under an assumed name in some of the Southern states. His prizes were given to Weislander.

In addition, Thorpe won the American all-around championship. At this time, Martin Sheridan, one of our greatest all-around champions, told me that in his estimation Thorpe was the best all-around athlete in the world, bar none. . . .

Thorpe could clear 6 feet 4½ inches in the running high jump, run a hundred yards in 10 seconds flat, pole vault over 11 feet, put the shot 44 feet 9 inches, cover 22 feet in the running broad jump, and 155 feet with the javelin, and run a fairly fast mile.

They told many stories about the big Indian on that Olympic trip to Stockholm. The King of Sweden, curious to see a real Indian at close quarters, sent Thorpe an invitation to dine with him. Thorpe declined the invitation, saying that he wanted to go to bed early. On leaving Sweden, Jim said the Swedes were fine sportsmen, and he enjoyed the trip, but he was anxious to get back to an American bath tub.[11]

Approach	Detail
Name	Jim Thorpe (Wa-Tho-Huk, Bright Path)
Age	At time of writing: 37 In 1912 (Olympics): 24
Gender (Connect to athletic events)	Male; compet4ed in men's football, baseball, and track and field. (Basketball is also mentioned in the Note.)
Nationality/Ethnic Group	American; mixed Native American and European ancestry; Sac Fox tribe

Appearance (Physical Characteristics)	
o Bodily Form	*Six feet tall, powerfully but lightly built, about 180 pounds*
o Physical Abilities	*Speed, natural ball handling ability, versatility, strong*
Mental State	*A "quick brain"; alert*
Emotional State	*Aggressive; modest; perhaps saddened when stripped of medals*

EXERCISE 2.2: Describing Appearance

Directions: On another piece of paper, write one paragraph describing a friend or family member. Use as many of the elements of appearance as possible: physical appearance, clothing, and manner. Elements of physical appearance include the following (though you can add more, if needed).

- o Body form
- o Facial expression
- o Voice
- o Posture
- o Physical abilities/disabilities

Tips for Writing Descriptions

Teachers in classical times gave their students tips for descriptive detail.

Tip #1:

The first tip for descriptive writing is to use *clear, specific* details so that the readers can better picture what is being described. Avoid vague and unclear details.

a. **Vague Details:** Phaia was not an ordinary pig.

   Specific Details: "Now the wild sow of Krommyon, whom they called Phaia, was no ordinary beast, but a fierce creature and hard to conquer" (Plutarch).[12]

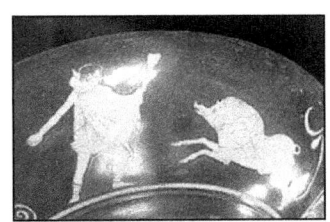

b. **Vague Details:** There was a man's coffin with a weapon beside it.

Specific Details: "There was found the coffin of a man of great stature, and lying beside it a brazen lance-head and a sword" (Plutarch).

EXERCISE 2.3: Examining Writing for Specific Details

Directions: Below are some sentences from *The Wizard of Oz* by Frank Baum (1856-1919). Baum's sentences are quite specific. In the exercise, each sentence is incomplete. You will see two possible ways to finish the sentence (A and B). In the blank, place the letter of the phrase which you think was written by Frank Baum, that is, the more descriptive phrase.

__A__ 1. When Dorothy was left alone she began to feel hungry. So she went to the cupboard and:
A. cut herself some bread, which she spread with butter.
B. got something to eat.

__B__ 2. Taking a pail from the shelf, she carried it down to the little brook and filled it with:
A. water. B. clear, sparkling water.

__B__ 3. There were several roads nearby, but it did not take her long to find:
A. the paved one.
B. the one paved with yellow bricks.

__A__ 4. As for the Scarecrow, having no brains, he walked straight ahead, and so stepped into the holes and:
A. fell at full length on the hard bricks.
B. fell down.

__B__ 5. The Lion said, "If . . . had ever tried to fight me, I should have run myself—I'm such a coward."
A. the other animals
B. the elephants and the tigers and the bears

EXERCISE 2.4: Choosing the Best Verb

Directions: Below are some sentences from the short story "To Build a Fire" by Jack London (1876-1916). In each sentence, one of London's strong words or phrases has been pulled out and appears with weaker words or phrases. In the blank, put the letter of the strongest word or phrase (i.e., the one London used).

__B__ 1. "He knew that a few more days must pass before that cheerful orb, due south, would just . . . above the skyline."

    A. rise   B. peep   C. appear

__A__ 2. "He thought of those biscuits, each cut open and . . . in bacon grease."

    A. sopped   B. placed   C. put

__C__ 3. "At the man's heels . . . a dog."

    A. came   B. was   C. trotted

__A__ 4. "He knew also that there were springs that . . . from the hillsides."

    A. bubbled up   B. came   C. ran

__C__ 5. Once, coming around a bend, he . . . abruptly, like a startled horse."

    A. stopped   B. discontinued   C. shied

EXERCISE 2.5: Writing Specific Details

Directions: Below you will see three illustrations from old-time books. Choose one of your classmates to go to the chalkboard as a scribe. Then together as a class, compose sentences with clear, specific words and strong verbs that help convey the mood of the situation. You may use the prompts as they are or change them by giving the characters names (e.g., Billy, Aunt Martha, etc.).

1. The girl with the basket . . . .

2. The girl on the gate . . . .

3. The boy . . . .

4. The man . . . .

5. The cat . . . .

6. The girl . . . .

7. The girl . . . .

8. Her brother . . . .

Tip #2:

The second tip for descriptive writing is to use figures of speech such as similes and metaphors. In the last chapter, similes were explained as comparisons using *like* or *as* ("Jesus said he was *like* a good shepherd.") Metaphors are another kind of comparison, but they do not use *like* or *as*. Rather, they use forms of *be* ("Jesus said, 'I *am* the good shepherd'").

a. **Simple statement:** This is a ship that turns up in the front.

Statement using a simile: "This is a ship having a beak turned up *like* a swine's snout" (Plutarch).

b. **Simple statement:** "I'm not the only one who lost his honor."

Statement using a metaphor: "I'm not the only fox without a tail" (Plutarch).

EXERCISE 2.6: Examining Writing for Similes and Metaphors

Directions: Below are some lines of poetry by the American poet Emily Dickinson (1830-1886). If the lines contain a simile, put an *S* in the blank. If they contain a metaphor, put an *M* in the blank.

M 1. "Hope" is the thing with feathers—
 That perches in the soul—

S 2. Like trains of cars on tracks of plush
 I hear the level bee:

_S_ 3. Departed to the judgment,
    A mighty afternoon;
    Great clouds like ushers leaning,
    Creation looking on.

_S_ 4. As children bid the guest good-night,
    And then reluctant turn,
    My flowers raise their pretty lips,
    Then put their nightgowns on.

_M_ 5. I shall know why, when time is over,
    And I have ceased to wonder why;
    Christ will explain each separate anguish
    In the fair schoolroom of the sky.

EXERCISE 2.7: Writing with Similes and Metaphors

Directions: Choose one of your classmates to go to the chalkboard as a scribe. Then, with your classmates, use the prompt to help you compose sentences with similes and metaphors to describe the people or the situations in the pictures. Copy into your book the statement the scribe records on the board.

1. The girl seems to be drawing on a wall. Compose a sentence using a phrase like *as quietly as* or *as impishly as*.

2. The children both seem to be having fun. Compose a sentence using a simile or a metaphor to describe their giggling.

3. Somebody has tipped a canoe. Compose a sentence with a simile (using *like* or *as*).

4. Somebody has riled up the bees. Compose a sentence using a simile or a metaphor.

Quills #1

Your teacher will give you the instructions you need to write a description of a person.

Topics for Describing Objects

When describing objects, focus on these topics:

a. Color

b. Size

c. Shape

d. Texture

e. Age

f. Material

g. Attribute

EXERCISE 2.8: Examining a Description of an Object

Directions: Please begin by reading the description of the colonial ship found at the site of the World Trade Center. Then, with your classmates, use the chart to help you identify the seven topics used to describe the ship.

Colonial Ship at Site of World Trade Center

Sloop.

In 2010, as construction workers were beginning the foundations for the new World Trade Center in New York, they discovered an eighteenth-century wooden ship buried 20 feet below the surface of the earth. The curved timbers had taken on the color of the grey muck in which they were buried. The ship measured 32 feet long, but archaeologists estimated that it was originally 50 feet long at the base and 60 feet long on the deck. They also noted that the ship was similar to the flat-bottomed sloop of the Dutch type. Its frame was made of white oak while traces of hickory were found in the keel. The rough, worm-eaten condition of the timbers was probably due to shipworms found in the warm saltwater of the Caribbean, where trade flourished in the eighteenth century. Archaeologists later examined the tree rings on the oak timber and determined that the trees which were used to build the ship had been cut down in about 1773.

Approach	Detail
Color	What color did the ship appear to be when it was discovered? *It had the color of the grey muck in which it was buried.*
Size	What was the length of the ship? Remains: *32 feet* Original Base: *50 feet* Original Deck: *60 feet*
Shape	What shape were the timbers? *The timbers were curved.*
Texture	How did the timbers feel to the touch? *Rough* What was probably the cause? *Worm holes (worms from Caribbean)*
Age	By examining the tree rings of the timber used to build the ship, archaeologists dated the origin of the ship to what year? *1773*
Material	What two materials were used to make the ship? Frame: *white oak* Keel: *hickory*
Attribute	Of what design was the ship? *It had the design of a Dutch sloop.*

EXERCISE 2.9: Examining a Description of an Object

 Directions: Please read the description of an American felling axe. Then complete the chart that follows.

The American Felling Axe

 One of the most useful tools to the American pioneer was the felling axe. This tool could be used to clear land and to build homes. An axe, then as now, consisted of two main parts: the axe head and the handle. In the last half of the nineteenth century, American axe heads were made of either iron, steel, or a combination of the two. The pioneer's axe head weighed from three to six pounds. When new, they had a smooth, forge-blackened finish, but over time, they would become scratched, nicked, or rusty. However, if the handle of the axe cracked or broke, the durable axe head could still be remounted on a new handle. The handle (or haft) was generally 30 to 36 inches in length. Traditionally, it was made of a resilient hardwood such as hickory or ash. In the 1840s, manufacturers began to make curved hafts, which gave a better grip and helped in the swinging motion.

Approach	Detail
Color	Head: *forge-blackened*
Size	Weight of head: *3-6 lb.* Length of haft: *30-36 in.*
Shape	Haft: *curved*
Texture	Head when new: *smooth* Head after use: *scratched, nicked, rusty*

Teacher's Edition

Age	Date of manufacture: *1870*
Material	Head: *iron, steel, or a combination* Haft: *hardwood such as hickory or ash*
Attribute	Advantage of curved haft: *better grip; helped in swinging motion*

EXERCISE 2.10: Writing Descriptions with Similes and Metaphors

 Directions: With a partner, compose descriptions using the prompts below. When everyone is finished, read your descriptions to the others in your class.

1. The ear pods for your iPhone do not work. Describe them in a way that shows your frustration.

2. You used a Sharpie to draw a picture for class, but the picture fell into the swimming pool. Describe its appearance when you pulled it out of the water.

3. A kindergartener has to find a way to get her sixth-grade brother's bicycle home from school. Describe the bike as it appears to the child.

4. An army of ants is carrying a feather. Describe the feather from the point of view of the ants.

5. Your aunt lives far away and has not seen you since you started school at age five. Describe the pajamas she sends you for a birthday gift.

Quills #2

 Your teacher will give you the instructions you need to write a Description of an object.

NARRATIVE

Chapter 3

Introduction

Have you ever told ghost stories around a camp fire? Or, do you have a father or grandfather who can keep you interested for hours with war stories? What do you talk about with your friends while eating in the lunch room? Chances are you talk about what happened that morning or the previous night. It seems that almost everywhere a person goes, narrative is a big part of conversation.

The ancient Greeks understood this great human love for stories. Their word *mūthos*, which means *report* or *story*, is the source of our word *myth*. In English, this word refers to a special category of story, one which has perhaps superhuman elements. For a more straightforward report of the facts without the elements of a tall tale, speakers of English use the word *narrative*, which comes from the Latin word *narrāre*, *to tell* or *to narrate*.

Because stories form the lion's share of what we talk about with each other, the teachers in ancient Greece chose to begin a student's education in composition with fables, myths, and narratives. These forms of writing are among the first few exercises of the progymnasmata. Moreover, as students move farther into the progymnasmata, the use of narrative is not left by the wayside. Rather, narrative plays a key role in almost every one of the exercises. In short, narrative is the foundation of classical composition.

Definition and Purpose of the Narrative

1. Narrative is defined as a story about something that happened in the past.

2. Narratives have many purposes.

   a. In the form of fiction, writers use them as entertainment.
   b. In the newspaper, journalists use them to communicate current events to the general public.
   c. In a courtroom, lawyers use them to explain a crime to a jury.
   d. In the classroom, teachers use them to explain human history.
   e. At church, pastors use them to help us understand God's plan.

 **THINK IT THROUGH:** Why do you think people enjoy stories so much? Why do you think we *need* stories so much?

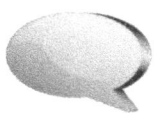 **THINK IT THROUGH:** What two narratives did Moses use to begin the book of Genesis? Why do you think that beginning with those narratives was better than starting with, say, definitions of *sin* and *salvation*?

Types of Narratives

One can find many types of narratives, but here we will discuss two: the mythical narrative and the historical narrative.

Type One: The Mythical Narrative

Characteristics

1. In ancient Greece and Rome, the mythical narrative was a tale or a legend about gods or heroes.

2. Like the fable, the mythical narrative can be used to teach a moral.

3. A mythical narrative differs from a fable in three ways:

   a. The characters are heroic humans, not animals or objects. In classical times, the characters sometimes included gods or goddesses as well.

   b. The characters normally have names.

   c. The stories often involve superhuman accomplishments.

   d. The moral to the story is not normally expressed at the end of the tale.

Model Mythical Narrative

Daedalus and Icarus

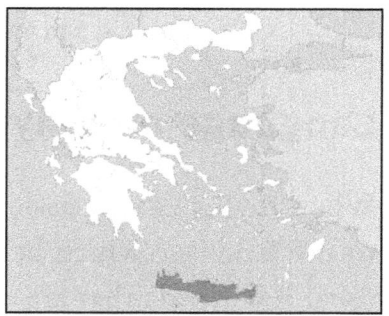

Daedalus was an Athenian architect, sculptor, and inventor. For a time, he was living in exile on the island of Crete where King Minos was happy to treat him with respect. One of Daedalus' most notable inventions was the famous maze of Crete. This maze was so full of intersecting passages that even Daedalus himself almost lost his way once!

In the course of time, the great inventor began to notice that during the day King Minos would always treat him like one of his worthies, but at the end of each day, would escort him back to the stone tower where Daedalus resided with his young son Icarus. He began to feel as though he and Icarus were prisoners. Therefore, he decided that the time had come for them to escape Crete and return home to Greece.

Now, Daedalus was a great inventor, but it took some thinking to dream up a device that would help Icarus and him make an escape. Since Crete was an island, Daedalus decided that the most comfortable passage to Athens would be by air.

Therefore, he set to work at once using feathers to construct two sets of wings—one for himself and the other for Icarus. He used wax to attach the wings to their arms.

Then, fearful for the boy's safety, Daedalus undertook to teach his son the art of flight. He would attach the wings to the boy's arms and take him to a cliff overlooking the sea.

Each time before the launch, he would advise his son, "Be careful, Icarus. Don't fly too high, because if you get too close to the sun, the wax will melt and you will fall." So, taking his father's instructions to heart, Icarus would launch into the warm air and fly upward as high as his father would allow, enjoying the thrill of floating with the clouds.

17th-Century depiction of Daedulus, Icarus, and the maze

But one day Icarus became so joyful in flight that he completely forgot his father's oft-repeated warning not to approach too near the sun. Alas, as his father had predicted, the wax that held everything together completely melted away and Icarus plunged earthward into the sea. It is said that the island called Icaria is named for the unfortunate lad Icarus.

Language of a Mythical Narrative

When myths from classical Greece and Rome are translated into English, the translators like to use language which helps to instill a sense of the past into the narrative. To do this, they use a few words that are no longer used in English. Old-fashioned or "quaint" words of this type are called *archaisms*. There are two archaisms in the last paragraph of the narrative of Daedalus and Icarus: the adverb *oft* (instead of *often*) and the interjection *alas* (which expresses sadness).

EXERCISE 3.1: Mythical Narrative

Directions: Answer the following questions about the legend "Daedulus and Icarus."

1. Which does the story concern: humans or gods?

   It concerns humans.

2. What skill does Daedulus possess that makes him almost "superhuman"?

   Daedulus is an incredible architect and inventor. He even makes a gigantic maze and a flying machine by himself.

Teacher's Edition

3. What do you consider to be the moral to this story?

Answers will vary, but students should recognize that Icarus' failure to heed wise advice led to his fall.

Mythical Narratives in America: The Tall Tale

The mythical narrative is not just a relic of the past. People still enjoy spinning yarns and telling *tall tales*, stories which include superhuman elements like lassoing the moon or leaping the Grand Canyon.

Perhaps the most famous figure from the tradition of the American tall tale is Paul Bunyan, a giant lumberjack of superhuman strength who originated amongst Wisconsin loggers. Also well known is Pecos Bill of the American Southwest (Texas, New Mexico, Arizona, and California). After the Civil War, the people of the United States were in the process of moving westward and building a nation, and these pioneers truly did exhibit amazing strength and determination against enormous challenges. Perhaps it is not surprising that their heroes were a bit larger than life as they cut the challenges down to size.

Model Tall Tale

Pecos Bill Rides a Tornado

Now, Pecos Bill could ride anything that ever was. So, as some tell the story, there came a storm bigger than any other. It all happened during the worst drought the West had ever seen. It was so dry that horses and cows started to dry up and blow away in the wind. So when Bill saw the windstorm, he got an idea. The huge tornado kicked across the land like a wild bronco. But Bill jumped on it without a thought.

He rode that tornado across Texas, New Mexico and Arizona, all the time squeezing the rain out of it to save the land from drought. When the storm was over, Bill fell off the tornado. He landed in California. He left a hole so deep that to this day it is known as Death Valley.[13]

 **THINK IT THROUGH:** How is the story "Pecos Bill Rides a Tornado" similar to the Greek myth "Daedalus and Icarus"? How is it different?

Characteristics of the American Tall Tale

1. **Setting:** The tall tale usually has a rural setting.

   a. Davy Crockett's tall tales were set in the mountains of his home state of Tennessee.

   b. The Paul Bunyan stories were set in the logging regions of Wisconsin.

   c. The Pecos Bill stories are set on the Plains or in the desert of the southwest.

2. **Characters:** The main characters are often larger-than-life men and women of superhuman strength who can easily handle the gigantic problems that faced the settlers.

3. **Techniques:**

   a. One technique of the tall tale is *hyperbole* (hī PER bə lē), which is the use of exaggeration to make a special effect. Here is one example:

   > "[Nance Bowers] had one of the most universally useful mouths in her face that ever fell to the head of humanity; she could eat victuals with one corner, whistle with the other, an' scream with the middle. . . ."[14]

   b. Another technique is the use of *simile* (SĬM ə lē), which is a comparison using *like* or *as*. Here are some examples:

   > "Every winter she fatted up on bear's meat, so that when she turned out in spring, she war bigger round than a whiskey barrel; and when I put my arms 'round the creatur, it war *like* hugging a bale of cotton."

   > "Seven men were kept busy with wheelbarrows hauling prune stones away from the camp. The chipmunks ate these and grew *as big as* tigers."

4. **Language:** The narrator uses "folksy" language. This technique tries to catch the dialect of the people who created the tale.[15]

   a. It includes spellings that represent the pronunciation of the people. For example, the word *for* might be spelled as *fer*. The word *against* might be spelled as *agin*. Here is an example from the Davy Crockett tales:

   > "This gal was named Jerusa Stubbs, and had only one eye, but that was pritty enough for two."

   b. The language might include non-standard English, what some people might call "bad grammar." That is because the stories originated with the practical people building the country, not the "city folk" of the East. Here is another example from the Davy Crockett tales:

   > "Then I seed I couldn't do nothing with my arms, for they war fastened by the snakes like ropes."

   c. Tall tale narrators might even make up a few words of their own, as in this Davy Crockett line:

   > "We had some of the most *ragiferous* fights with Alligators."

EXERCISE 3.2: Examining a Tall Tale

 <u>Directions</u>: Below is one of the most famous tales about Paul Bunyan. Please read the tale and answer the questions that follow.

The Blue Ox

Bunyan was assisted in his lumbering by a huge blue ox of whom he was very fond. This ox had the strength of nine horses and it weighed ten thousand pounds. It measured seven axe handles between the eyes. Its horns were of immense size. The men tied a line to their tips and hung clothing on it to dry. The original color of the animal was pure white. One winter it snowed blue snow for seven days and the ox lying down in it all winter was dyed blue. With the ox Paul dragged a whole house up a hill, then he dragged the cellar up after it. When he wanted to peel a log he hitched the ox to one end and himself took hold of the bark at the other. The ox pulled and out came the log "as clean as a whistle." The ox sometimes got into mischief. Once he broke loose at night and ate up two hundred feet of tow line. Sometimes he slipped in behind the crew, drank the water in the river and left the drive high and dry. Some of the lakes in Wisconsin and Minnesota are in holes made by his feet. Bunyan had many other oxen. When strung out in a line, if each took the tail of the other in his mouth, they would stretch halfway across the state. Their yokes piled up made one hundred cords of wood. One day he drove his oxen through a hollow log which had fallen across a great ravine. When they came through he counted them and saw that several were missing. These, he found, had strayed into a hollow limb.[16]

Questions:

1. Underline one example of hyperbole. *(Almost every sentence contains hyperbole.)*

2. Write down at least one example of superhuman (or in this case "superanimal") strength from this tale.

    Any example can be accepted.

3. Write down an example of colloquial language.

    The log came out "as clean as a whistle."

4. The language in this tale contains only one example of non-standard English. What grammar mistake appears in this sentence?

    ". . . he hitched the ox to one end and himself took hold of the bark at the other."

    The word himself is not proper in the subject position. Here it is the subject of the verb took hold.

Quills #1: Writing a Tall Tale

 Your teacher will provide you with a composition assignment so that you can show your ability to write a Tall Tale.

Teacher's Edition

Type Two: The Historical Narrative

Characteristics

1. The historical narrative tells about an important event in the past.

2. It is often used at times of celebration, such as the Thanksgiving narrative of the Pilgrims.

3. Like the fable and the mythical narrative, the historical narrative can teach a lesson about life.

THINK IT THROUGH: What patriotic narratives are associated with Independence Day (the Fourth of July)? What Bible narratives are associated with Christian holidays?

Model Historical Narrative

The Bald Knobbers: Taney County Vigilantes

[1] In the two decades following the Civil War, the western states were plagued with lawlessness. With few courts or lawmen to keep the peace, residents in a troubled area would often appoint themselves to track down and punish outlaws. These trackers were known as *vigilance committees* or, sometimes, just as *vigilantes*. However, sometimes the vigilantes went overboard and became as bad as those they set out to eliminate.

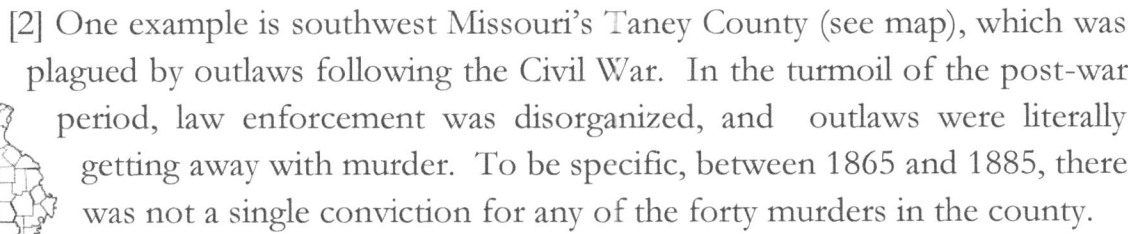

[2] One example is southwest Missouri's Taney County (see map), which was plagued by outlaws following the Civil War. In the turmoil of the post-war period, law enforcement was disorganized, and outlaws were literally getting away with murder. To be specific, between 1865 and 1885, there was not a single conviction for any of the forty murders in the county.

Narrative | 37

[3] In 1883, a fellow named Nathaniel "Nat" Kinney moved his family into the area and became very concerned about the violence there. After another murder went unpunished in autumn that year, Kinney gathered together twelve other men and began to hold secret meetings on a hill, or "knob," called Snapp's Bald, which was just north of Kirbyville. Because of this meeting place, they came to be called the Bald Knobbers.

[4] Their group became emboldened as it grew larger, and in April of 1885, they dragged two outlaws out of jail and hanged them. Though some members dropped out after this, the Bald Knobbers actually grew, becoming a 1,000-member vigilante group. As their strength in numbers grew, they began to expand their tactics beyond law and order and undertook campaigns against social ills such as wife beating, gambling, and drinking. Wearing muslin masks with holes cut out for nose, eyes, and mouth, they would go after men who owed them money and would even hang people for infractions such as disturbing the peace or vandalizing property. People who spoke out against them would turn up dead, the victims of beatings.

Depiction of Bald Knobbers from the movie *The Shepherd of the Hills,* 1919

[5] Most of the Bald Knobbers had sided with the Union in the Civil War, but since Missouri had actually been a Confederate state, it was only natural that a group of Anti-Bald Knobbers also got up. This group's most well-known member was a nineteen-year-old orphan named Andy Coggburn. Coggburn's vicious hatred of the Bald Knobbers did not stop them, however, and Kinney murdered Coggburn "in self-defense" outside a church in Forsyth, Missouri.

[6] Kinney himself met a violent end in August 1888 when a farmer named Billy Miles killed him with three shots from a pistol. Like many an outlaw whom Kinney had earlier organized to rein in, Miles was not convicted for the murder. After Kinney's death, the vigilante group lost steam and within a year had collapsed. The long period of violence from before, during, and after the Civil War was at last brought to a close in Taney County.

EXERCISE 3.3: Examining a Historical Narrative

Directions: Please answer the questions below about "The Bald Knobbers: Taney County Vigilantes."

Teacher's Edition

1. The narrative does not really begin until Paragraph 2. What seems to be the purpose of Paragraph 1?

   Paragraph 1 provides background information to help the reader understand the narrative better.

2. Historical narratives are sometimes entertaining, but their primary purpose is to explain why things happened in the past. Please focus on causes in these questions:

   a. Why was law enforcement weak in this time period?

   After the Civil War, the area was disorganized.

   b. Why did Nat Kinney originally organize his group?

   He originally organized the group to bring order to the area.

   c. Why was Kinney's group called the "Bald Knobbers"?

   They took their name from the place where they met.

   d. What caused the decline of the Bald Knobbers in 1888?

   The murder of Nat Kinney caused the decline of the group.

3. Like fables, narratives can help teach a lesson. What do you think is the lesson of this narrative?

   Answers will vary, but the narrative shows how vigilante groups might begin with good intentions but grow violent.

Six Elements of the Narrative

Teachers in classical times identified the six elements of a narrative in this way:

Agent
Action
Time
Place
Cause
Manner

Narrative | 39

Fortunately, speakers of English have found an easier way to remember these elements, listing them as question words, thus:

Who?
What?
When?
Where?
Why?
How?

 **THINK IT THROUGH:** As a class, return to the story "The Bald Knobbers: Taney County Vigilantes." On the board, specify each of the elements:

a. Who was the main character in the narrative? *Nat Kinney*
b. What did the main character do? *Organized vigilantes to bring order to the area*
c. When did the action take place? *1883-1888*
d. Where did the action take place? *Taney County, Missouri*
e. Why was law enforcement disorganized in this time and place? *Civil War*
f. How did the vigilantes punish wrongdoers? *They hanged them.*

 **EXERCISE 3.4: Elements of Narrative**

Directions: On a piece of notebook paper, write the title of a book or a movie with which you are familiar. Then list its various elements.

a. Who were the main characters?
b. What happened in the story?
c. When did the story take place?
d. Where did the story take place?
e. Why did the action in the story happen?
f. How did the main character solve his/her problem?

Retelling a Narrative

Sometimes in life we need the skill of retelling a narrative. In classical times, teachers taught several ways to do that. Here we will look at two of them.

Shortening a Narrative

Often in school, teachers ask students to write a book report. The best book reports are those that focus on the six basic elements listed above: who, what, when, where, why, and how. This is called writing a *summary*. Another way to refer to a summary is to call it a *shortened narrative*.

Model Shortened Narrative

The Chisholm Trail
(Original Narrative: 137 Words)

The Chisholm Trail was the most important route for cattle drives leading north from Fort Worth, Texas, across Indian Territory (now Oklahoma) to the railhead at Abilene, Kansas. It was about 520 miles long but never had an exact location, as different drives took somewhat different paths. Farmers often complained about the Texas longhorns because they carried ticks that caused disease in their cattle. Therefore, Texas cattlemen needed a trail that would skirt the farm settlements, avoiding the trouble over tick fever. In 1867 a livestock dealer named Joseph G. McCoy built market facilities at Abilene, Kansas, where the Chisholm Trail ended. Soon a herd of 2,400 steers made the cattle drive northward from Texas to Abilene. By the time the traffic on the trail diminished in 1871, about 5,000,000 head of cattle had made that trip.

The Chisholm Trail
(Shortened Narrative: 68 words)

The Chisholm Trail was the main route for driving cattle from the ranches of Fort Worth, Texas, to the railroad at Abilene, Kansas, from 1867 to 1871. It was a 520-mile long trail which started west of settled areas since farmers were concerned about disease-carrying ticks.

Livestock dealer Joseph G. McCoy headed up the market at Abilene, bringing up 5,000,000 cattle during the trail's four years of operation.

Paraphrasing

When teachers make assignments, they often say, "Please write the report in your own words." Writing something in your own words is very important for two reasons:

a. It helps the teacher to see that the student has indeed understood the reading.

b. It helps the student steer clear of the charge of cheating. In the United States, copying someone else's words is considered the same as "stealing" from them. However, summarizing a piece of writing in one's own words is considered fair to both the author and reader.

Example:

Original: "Farmers often complained about the Texas longhorns because they carried ticks that caused disease in their cattle."

Paraphrase: *Farmers were upset about the disease-carrying ticks on Texas longhorns.*

Techniques of Paraphrasing

There are several specific changes you can make to put a sentence into your own words.

1. Use a synonym, usually an easier word.

   "The summer heat was *severe*"

   ➤ The summer heat was *harsh*.

2. Omit information that is not necessary. (Note: By itself, this technique would not result in a complete paraphrase.

   The Chisholm Trail needed to intersect with rivers, *such as the Arkansas River in Wichita, Kansas,* so that the men, cattle, and horses could be provided with water.

> "The Chisholm Trail needed to intersect with rivers so that the men, cattle, and horses could drink water."

3. Change the sentence structure. For example, you can change a noun to a verb or *vice versa*.

   "In 1867, the first cattle *drive* north involved 35,000 head of cattle."

   > In 1867, 35,000 head of cattle *were driven* north.

EXERCISE 3.5: Examining Paraphrase

Directions: Following are sentences from the original narrative about the Chisholm Trail with some parts underlined. Look in the shortened narrative to find out how the underlined part was paraphrased and copy the re-phrasing in the space provided. The first one serves as an example.

1. **Original:**

   "The Chisholm Trail was the most important route for cattle drives. . . ."

   Paraphrase:

   . . . the main route . . .

2. **Original:**

   ". . . route for cattle drives leading north from Fort Worth, Texas, across Indian Territory (now Oklahoma) to the railhead at Abilene, Kansas."

   Paraphrase: *from the ranches of Fort Worth, Texas, to the railroad at Abilene, Kansas*

3. **Original:**

   "It was about 520 miles long. . . ."

   Paraphrase: *It was a 520-mile long trail.*

4. **Original:**

"... <u>a livestock dealer named Joseph G. McCoy built market facilities</u> at Abilene, Kansas, where the Chisholm Trail ended."

Paraphrase: *Livestock dealer Joseph G. McCoy opened up the cattle market at Abilene, Kansas.*

EXERCISE 3.6: Paraphrase Practice

<u>Directions</u>: Read the original sentences, which are based on information in *Wikipedia*. Then practice putting the information into your own words. The first one serves as an example.

1. "The original English word for *cowboy* was *cowherd*, which was similar to *shepherd*, and referred to a boy in early adolescence."

    ❖ What is another way of saying "a boy in early adolescence"?

    "a boy about twelve to fourteen years old"

2. "Another English word for a cowboy, *buckaroo*, is an Anglicization of the Spanish word *vaquero*, which comes from the Latin word *vacca*, meaning *cow*."

    ❖ What is another way of saying that *buckaroo* is an "Anglicization" of a Spanish word?

    The English word <u>buckaroo</u> comes from a Spanish word.

3. "A subtype of cowboy, called a *wrangler*, specifically tended the horses used to work cattle."

    ❖ What is another way of saying "subtype"?

    Answers will vary, but "another type" would suffice

    ❖ What is another way of saying a wrangler "tended the horses"?

    He took care of the horses.

Teacher's Edition

4. "The term *cowgirl* first appeared in the late nineteenth century."

   ❖ What is another way of saying it "first appeared"? *It was first used*

   ❖ What is another way of saying "the late nineteenth century"?

   near the end of the 1800's

5. "Synonyms for the word *cowboy* are *cowhand*, which appeared in 1852, and *cowpoke*, which appeared in 1881."

   ❖ Re-write this sentence omitting the adjective clauses, which indicate the dates when the synonyms first appeared.

   Synonyms for the word <u>cowboy</u> are <u>cowhand</u> and <u>cowpoke</u>.

   ❖ Is there another way to say "synonyms . . . are"?

   ❖ *a. Other words for . . . are . . . .*
   ❖ *b. Another way to say . . . is . . . .*

EXERCISE 3.7: Retelling a Narrative

Directions: Below is a short historical narrative about the Battle of Beecher's Island. After reading the narrative, identify the six basic elements of the narrative by filling out the chart. Then write a retelling of the narrative in your own words.

The Battle of Beecher Island
September 17, 1868

In the summer and fall of 1868, the Cheyenne Indians had been making attacks on settlers and trains in the area of Fort Wallace near the Kansas-Colorado border. The army was spread so thin on the frontier that Colonel George Alexander "Sandy" Forsyth recruited fifty hardy frontiersmen to help him seek out the Cheyenne and engage them in battle. Forsyth's party set out on September 16 and camped for the night in Yuma County, Colorado. With them was Lt. Frederick Beecher, a nephew of the famous brother and sister, clergyman Henry Ward Beecher and author Harriet Beecher Stowe. At dawn, on September 17, Chief Roman Nose and his Cheyenne warriors attempted a surprise attack. Against Forsyth's group of only fifty men, Chief Roman Nose brought hundreds of Cheyenne. Estimates vary from 600 to 1,000 warriors. Forsyth's men took cover on a small island (or sandbar) in the river, and the fight was on. Though outnumbered at least twelve to one, the frontiersmen still stood a chance since they were armed with Spencer repeating rifles, which could shoot seven rounds without being reloaded. Forsyth told the men with him on the island not to fire until the Indians' ponies reached the water, while three scouts who had remained near the camp were able to shoot from their hiding spot in a depression on the riverbank. When Chief Roman Nose was felled, the Indians retreated, leaving behind seventy five dead.

Amazed, one of the scouts remarked, "I have been on these plains, boy and man, for twenty years and I never saw anything like it."[17] Only eighteen of Forsyth's fifty men survived and all, including Forsyth, were wounded, some seriously. Beecher, for whom the island was later named, was among the dead. Forsyth sent scouts to Colonel Henry Bankhead at Fort Wallace, seeking assistance. The men had to sustain themselves on rotting horse flesh, cactus, and muddy river water, but the few remaining had enough ammunition to protect themselves for eight more days until relief finally arrived on September 25. Ultimately, When General George Armstrong Custer wrote his autobiography in 1874, he described the battle in detail and commented that, considering how greatly Forsyth's men were outnumbered, the Battle of Beecher Island was "one of the most remarkable and at the same time successful contests in which our forces on the Plains have ever been engaged."[18]

Identify the basic elements of the narrative in the chart below. Then on another piece of paper, retell the narrative of the Battle of Beecher Island in your own words, writing directly from the details on the chart without looking at the original.

Element	Details
Who?	Participants: *Col. George Forsyth, U.S. Army; 50 frontiersmen; Lt. Frederick Beecher; 600 Cheyenne Indians; Chief Roman Nose* Number of surviving whites still from total of 50: *19, including Forsyth* Number of Indians killed: *75*

Teacher's Edition

What?	Name of battle: *Battle of Beecher Island* Result of battle: *The Cheyenne scattered and Forsyth's men held out for nine days.*
When?	Date of departure: *September 16, 1868* Date of letter for help: *September 18* Date of attack: *September 17* Date of rescue: *September 25*
Where?	Name and location of fort: *Fort Wallace, near Kansas-Colorado border* Location of battle: *sandbar on Arikaree River, a tributary to North Fork of Republican River, Yuma County, Colorado*
Why?	Reason Custer called the battle "remarkable" and "successful"? *Though greatly outnumbered, Forsyth's men held out for nine days.*
How?	Weapons: *Spencer and Henry rifles* Means of survival until rescue: *horse flesh, cactus, muddy river water*

Quills #2: Writing a Historical Narrative

 Your teacher will provide you with a composition assignment so that you can show your ability to write a Historical Narrative.

WRITING A GOOD PARAGRAPH

Chapter 4

Introduction

Have you ever heard someone say, "Stop beating around the bush and get to the point!" This common complaint about the way people sometimes communicate goes to the heart of the way information is packaged in the English-speaking world.

In some parts of the world, it is considered polite to have a long lead-in to the main point, often with what we consider "flowery" language that is nice but not really necessary.

In other parts of the world, speakers and writers use frequent repetition. Perhaps they are trying to make much of a point so that people do not forget the information, but, again, in the English-speaking world, repetition is considered wasteful of time and ink.

"Beating around the bush" has been perceived as a useless way to communicate since about 1400 when a medieval poet wrote this line in a story about the hero Generydes, who says:

> "But as it hath be sayde full long agoo,
> Some bete the bussh and some the byrdes take."[19]

["But as it has been said so long ago,
  Some beat the bush, and some the birds do take."]

In other words, if a person is trying to capture a bird in a bush, it is better just to take the bird than to beat the bush where they are perched, which accomplishes little. Similarly, when communicating, it is better to make direct statements than just to drop a few hints.

For this reason, English-speakers have long used a system of communication which is direct and clear. The purpose of this chapter is to introduce this age-old pattern of communication in English.

Purpose and Definitions

1. The organization pattern introduced in this chapter is used to communicate factual information to people. It is not for a narrative, which you practiced in the first three chapters of this book. Instead, it goes by the name *expository writing*. The word *expository* comes from the Latin word *expōnere*, which means *to explain, to set forth*. Therefore, paragraphs that explain something or set forth new information are called *expository paragraphs*.

2. A *paragraph* can be defined as a group of sentences that explain one idea. That idea is set forth in the first sentence of the paragraph, *the topic sentence*. Then the rest of the paragraph explains it.

3. Just as no one wants to get lost in the woods, so no one wants to get lost in someone else's words! Therefore, as we write paragraphs in English, we use certain words to help guide readers through the information. Some examples are words like *first*, *second*, and *last*. These words are called *transitions*.

4. The word *transition* comes from the Latin word *transīre*, which means *to go across*. So as travelers might go across, or transit, a desert, readers "go across," or "transit," a paragraph. Just as road signs help travelers, so transition words help readers navigate their way through a paragraph.

Model Paragraph

Let's begin by looking at a finished paragraph and then showing the process used to create it. Imagine a situation where a social studies teacher asked the students to select a product they like and do some research about the sale of the product overseas. One student, whom we will call Rafe, selected Coca Cola as his favorite product and did some reading in the library or online about the Coca Cola Company's sales program. Below is a copy of the paragraph he ultimately wrote and turned in to the teacher:

(1) The Coca Cola Company has developed different flavors to sell in different parts of the world. (2) One such flavor is called *Citra* because it is flavored with lemon and lime, which are citrus fruits. (3) This flavor has been popular in Mexico, Japan, and New Zealand since 2006. (4) Another product marketed overseas is Coca Cola Orange. (5) This flavor was introduced in the United Kingdom and Gibraltar in 2007 but is now available in Gibraltar, Latvia, and Russia. (6) The last of the overseas Coke products is Coca Cola Blāk, which is coffee-flavored (7) This product has been particularly popular in the eastern European countries of the Czech Republic, Bosnia and Herzegovina, Bulgaria, and Lithuania. (8) In conclusion, Coke is available in different flavors in various countries around the world.

In this paragraph, Rafe has used the standard direct method of English paragraph writing. In the next few sections, we will examine the methods Rafe used to compose this paragraph and then do some practice.

Topic Sentence

When writing a paragraph in English, the first thing writers must do is identify the topic and the specific thing they want to say about the topic. These two components are called the *general idea (GT)* and the *controlling idea (CI)*, and together they make up the *topic sentence (TS)*.

Topic Sentence = General Topic + Controlling Idea

In Rafe's case, he wrote about the way the Coca Cola Company sells different flavors of Coca Cola in different parts of the world, which would break down this way:

General Topic = Coca Cola Company

Controlling Idea = Different flavors in different countries

Using these two parts, he wrote his topic sentence:

Topic Sentence = The Coca Cola Company has developed different flavors to sell in different parts of the world.

In conclusion, a topic sentence consists of two main parts: the general topic and the controlling idea.

EXERCISE 4.1: Identifying General Topic and Controlling Idea

Directions: In the topic sentences below, place the letters *GT* above the general topic and the letters *CI* above the controlling idea. The first one serves as an example.

1. The <u>planets of the solar system</u> can be divided into two main <u>types</u>.
                GT   *CI*

2. <u>Hot air balloons</u> carry several <u>forms of safety equipment</u>.
      GT   *CI*

3. Over the centuries, <u>animals</u> have <u>assisted humans</u> in many ways.
                       GT   *CI*

4. The <u>Appalachian Mountains</u> have three <u>main regions</u>.
         GT   *CI*

5. <u>German shepherds</u> are subject to three specific <u>health problems</u>.
     GT   *CI*

6. <u>Books in the library</u> can be divided into three <u>categories</u>.
       GT   *CI*

Teacher's Edition

Writing a Conclusion

At the end of a paragraph, writers frequently add a one-sentence conclusion. One way to think of a conclusion is to view it as an echo of the topic sentence. That is, like the topic sentence, the conclusion re-states the main idea and the controlling idea. Its purpose is to sum up everything to drive home the main idea at the end of the paragraph.

In Rafe's paragraph about flavors of Coca Cola, notice how the topic sentence (#1) and the conclusion (#8) have three similarities and three differences.

(1) The Coca Cola Company has developed different flavors to sell in different parts of the world. (2) One such flavor is called *Citra* because it is flavored with lemon and lime, which are citrus fruits. (3) This flavor has been popular in Mexico, Japan, and New Zealand since 2006. (4) Another product marketed overseas is Coca Cola Orange. (5) This flavor was introduced in the United Kingdom and Gibraltar in 2007 but is now available in Gibraltar, Latvia, and Russia. (6) The last of the overseas Coke products is Coca Cola Blāk, which is coffee-flavored (7) This product has been particularly popular in the eastern European countries of the Czech Republic, Bosnia and Herzegovina, Bulgaria, and Lithuania. **(8) In conclusion, Coke is available in various countries around the world in special flavors, such as Citra, Orange, and Blāk.**

<u>Similarities</u>:
a. Both are general (that is, they have no details).
b. Both state the general topic (the Coca Cola Company).
c. Both state the controlling idea (flavors around the world):

<u>Differences</u>:
a. The conclusion begins with a transition.
b. The sentences use slightly different wording.
c. *Optional:* The specific points (the three flavors) are named.

 **THINK IT THROUGH:** What is the transition in Sentence #8? Why do you think it is a good idea to use such a transition?

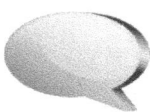 **THINK IT THROUGH:** Below are four phrases from Sentence #1 (the topic sentence). In the space provided, indicate how it is re-worded in Sentence #8 (the conclusion). The first one serves as an example.

In the blank for each Sentence 8, write the re-wording of the phrase from Sentence 1 above it.

a. Sentence #1 _Coca Cola_

   Sentence #8 _Coke_

b. Sentence #1 _has developed_

   Sentence #8 _is available_

c. Sentence #1 _different parts of the world_

   Sentence #8 _various countries around the world_

d. Sentence #1 _different flavors_

   Sentence #8 _special flavors, such as Citra, Orange, and Blak_

Paragraphs That List

There is one more thing to say about information paragraphs: they are often organized as lists. For that reason, the topic sentence will typically have a word that suggests a list is to follow. This word, which we will call a *listing signal*, could be a specific number such as *two* or *three*, or it could be an indefinite word such as *several* or *many*. Words of this type tip off the reader that a list is to follow. Here are some examples of topic sentences for the list type of paragraph:

   a. There are *three* changes I would like to make to my room.

   b. Mark Twain remains a popular American author for *several* reasons.

   c. Trees can be classified into *two* main types.

EXERCISE 4.2: Finding Listing Signals

 Directions: The sentences from Exercise 4.1 are reprinted below. Underline the listing signal in each one. Again, the first one serves as an example.

1. The planets of the solar system can be divided into <u>two</u> main types.

2. Hot air balloons carry <u>several</u> forms of safety equipment.

3. Over the centuries, animals have assisted humans in <u>many</u> ways.

4. The Appalachian Mountains have <u>three</u> main regions.

5. German shepherd dogs are subject to <u>three</u> specific health problems.

6. Books in the library can be divided into <u>two</u> main categories.

Zigzag Organization (from General to Specific)

Have you ever played the game called Categories? In this game, players slap their laps and clap their hands to create a rhythm. The leader throws out a general category. Then every time the fingers are snapped, a player takes a turn to name a specific member of that category. Here is an example:

Slap *Slap* / *Clap* *Clap*

    Snap *Snap* GROUP: Categories!

Slap *Slap* / *Clap* *Clap*

    Snap *Snap* GROUP: Such as!

Slap *Slap* / *Clap* *Clap*

    Snap *Snap* LEADER: Classroom items!

Slap *Slap* / *Clap* *Clap*

    Snap *Snap* PLAYER A: Globes!

Slap *Slap* / *Clap* *Clap*

    Snap *Snap* **PLAYER B: Dictionaries!**

Slap *Slap* / *Clap* *Clap*

    Snap *Snap* **PLAYER C: Desks!**

The game continues in this way until a player cannot think of another specific member of the category.

The Categories game illustrates how a paragraph is organized in English. In short, we start with the more general statement (*classroom items*) and then move to the more specific topic (e.g., *globes*).

In Rafe's paragraphs, his first two sentences are as follows:

> (1) The Coca Cola Company has developed different flavors to sell in different parts of the world. (2) One such flavor is called *Citra* because it is flavored with lemon and lime, which are citrus fruits.

Notice that Rafe has moved from general to specific. Sentence 1 is the more general statement because it refers to "different flavors," in general, and "different parts of the world," in general. It does not name any specific flavors or regions.

Sentence 2, however, is more specific because it specifically names Citra. Thus, Rafe has correctly moved from general (Sentence 1) to specific (Sentence 2).

Now, it is not enough for Rafe just to tell the name of the product. Since he mentioned "different parts of the world" in his topic sentence, he must now tell where Citra is sold. Therefore, Rafe uses Sentence 3 to add a *more* specific detail:

> (1) The Coca Cola Company has developed different flavors to sell in different parts of the world. (2) One such flavor is called *Citra* because it is flavored with lemon and lime, which are citrus fruits. (3) This flavor has been popular in Mexico, Japan, and New Zealand since 2006.

A scheme of the listing method looks like this:

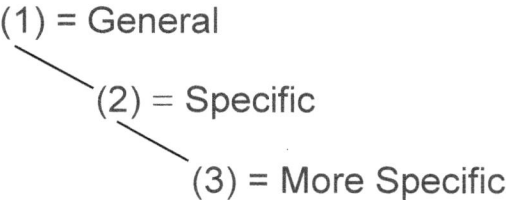

If we insert the information from Rafe's paper, the scheme looks like this:

But Citra was just Rafe's first point. Having given that point and its detail, he was ready to move to his second point, Coca Cola Orange, and the detail about that product. Then he added his third point and its detail. When finished, the complete scheme looked like the one on the next page.

THINK IT THROUGH: Notice in this scheme that after the movement from Sentence 1 to Sentence 2, the remainder of the sentences take a zigzag pattern. That is, they zig and zag as they move from specific to more specific. For this reason, we will call this pattern the *zigzag organization* of the English paragraph, or the "zigzag paragraph" for short.

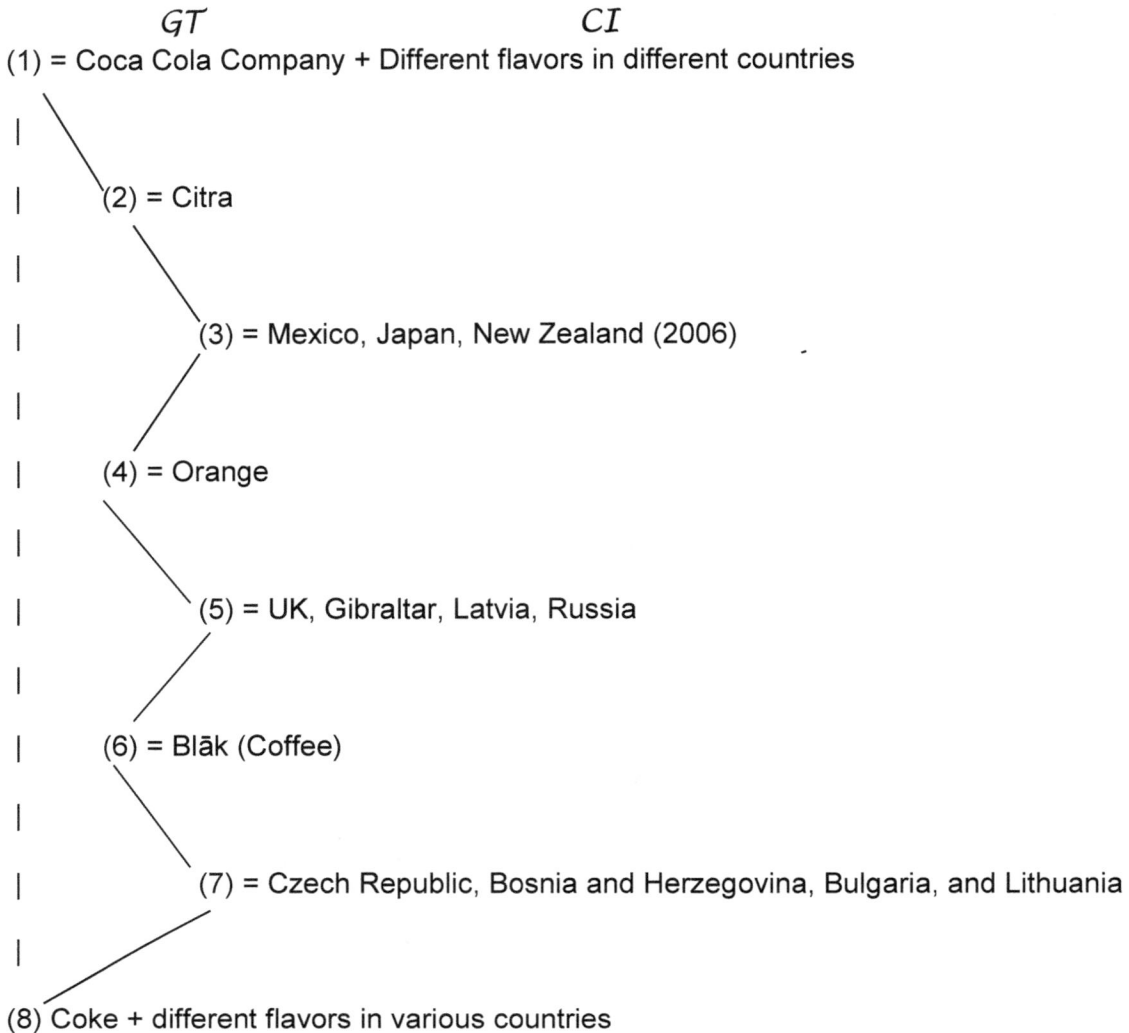

In this paragraph, Rafe has a topic sentence, three points, and one detail for each point for a total of seven sentences. Sentence 1 is the most general sentence, the topic sentence. Sentences 2, 4, and 6 are the main points. Sentences 3, 5, and 7 are the details.

When making a zigzag scheme for a paragraph that contains a conclusion, the number of the concluding sentence (in this case #8) must appear in line with the number of the topic sentence (#1). That is because they are both general. (Note the position of the numbers 1 and 8.)

Similarly, numbers 2, 4, and 6 line up because they mark the main points, and numbers 3, 5, and 7 line up because the mark the details.

EXERCISE 4.3: Analyzing a Scheme

Directions: To firm these techniques in your memory, please do the following to the scheme on the previous page:

1. Put the letter G above the numbers 1 and 8, because these numbers mark the GENERAL sentences.

2. Put the letter P above the numbers 2, 4, and 6, because these numbers mark the POINTS.

3. Put the letter D above the numbers 3, 5, and 7, because these numbers mark the DETAILS.

4. To the left of Sentences 2, 4, 6, and 8, write the transition word that introduces the sentence.

EXERCISE 4.4: Analyzing "Zigzag" Paragraphs

Directions: Please begin by reading the sample paragraph. Then complete the scheme that follows.

Dogs that Represent American Life

(1) Over the years, several dogs have become important representations of American life. (2) First, the Jack Russell Terrier named Nipper became famous in 1898 in a painting called *His Master's Voice*. (3) Nipper is pictured looking into the "horn" of the gramophone, with his head cocked, cleverly trying to figure out where his master's voice is coming from. (4) Second, the Cairn Terrier Toto was made famous in the 1939 movie *The Wizard of Oz*, a tale about a Kansas girl and her dog who are whisked away by a tornado to the Land of Oz. (5) In the story, Toto is a heroic character who helps Dorothy escape from the witch's castle. (6) Last, the collie Lassie, which originated in a novel set in Scotland, became an American symbol in the TV show *Lassie* (1954-73). (7) Lassie won hearts as the American farm dog that could save the day whenever a member of the family was in some kind of danger. (8) In conclusion, over the years the spirit of America has become symbolized in three famous pooches—Nipper, Toto, and Lassie.

Scheme:

Below you will see the scheme for "Dogs that Represent American Life." Some parts of the scheme are shown, but others are not. Please complete the scheme by putting key words or phrases from the paragraph into the blanks. When finished, connect the numbers with the zigzag lines and copy the transitions into the blanks in the left margin.

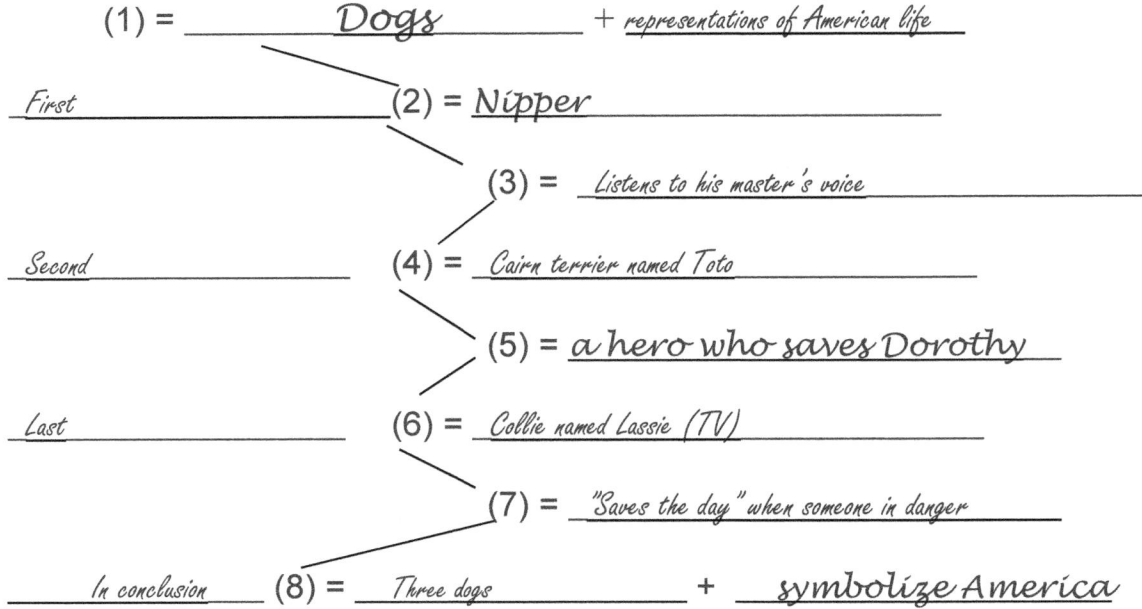

(1) = ___Dogs___ + ___representations of American life___

First _____ (2) = ___Nipper___

(3) = ___Listens to his master's voice___

Second _____ (4) = ___Cairn terrier named Toto___

(5) = ___a hero who saves Dorothy___

Last _____ (6) = ___Collie named Lassie (TV)___

(7) = ___"Saves the day" when someone in danger___

___In conclusion___ (8) = ___Three dogs___ + ___symbolize America___

EXERCISE 4.5: Analyzing a "Zigzag" Paragraph

 Directions: Please read the paragraph below. Then complete the scheme that follows.

Helpful NASA Inventions

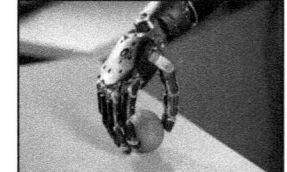

(1) The National Aeronautics and Space Administration (NASA) has invented several items that help ordinary folks here on earth. (2) One example is the so-called "space blanket," a light-weight plastic sheet which reflects heat. (3) These are often packed in first-aid kits to help accident victims keep warm. (4) Another example is the NASA helmet visor, which resists scratching. (5) The Foster-Grant company used this technology in its scratch-resistant sunglasses. (6) A third example is the invention of robots that can manipulate objects on the

outside of the spacecraft. (7) This research led to the development of artificial arms and legs for people who have lost limbs in accidents or war (see image). 8) In short, items that developed from the space program have improved our lives.

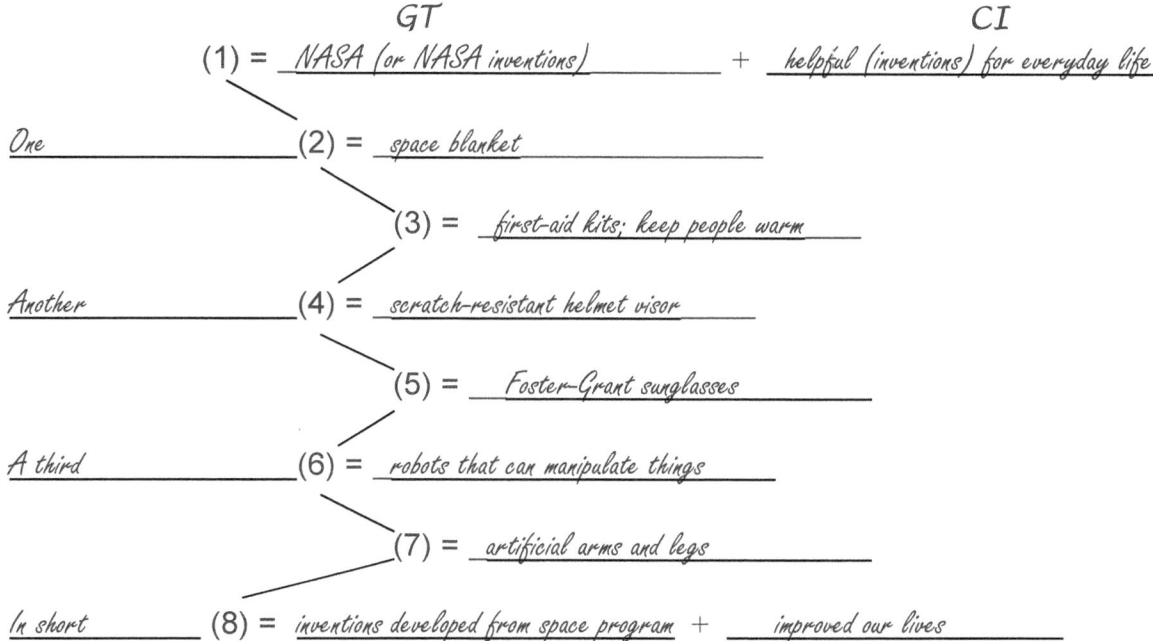

```
                                    GT                                    CI
              (1) = __NASA (or NASA inventions)__  + __helpful (inventions) for everyday life__
One           (2) = __space blanket__
              (3) = __first-aid kits; keep people warm__
Another       (4) = __scratch-resistant helmet visor__
              (5) = __Foster-Grant sunglasses__
A third       (6) = __robots that can manipulate things__
              (7) = __artificial arms and legs__
In short      (8) = __inventions developed from space program__ + __improved our lives__
```

EXERCISE 4.6: Creating a Zigzag Scheme

 Directions: Follow the steps below to create your own zigzag scheme.

1. Break the class into small groups of three or four students.

2. Decide on one thing all members of your group have in common. You can choose from the list below or create your own topic.

   Possible Topics:
   Sports
   Vacation spots
   Books
   Cooking
   (Your choice)

3. The general topic will be *group members*. The controlling idea will be whatever you discover to be the thing your group's members have in common. Those will both appear beside the number 1 (see scheme at right).

4. Then go on to complete a zigzag scheme for your group and topic similar to the one at the right. (If you have a group of four students, add an extra point and detail.)

5. After you have created your scheme, take it home and write up the paragraph. Do not forget to include the listing signals (*first, second, third,* etc.) and a concluding sentence.

(1) = Group members + pets
    (2) = Jenna
        (3) = dog Muff
    (4) = Rett
        (5) = cat Blinky
    (6) = Madison
        (7) = parrot Radar
(8) = All of us + own a pet

Quills #1: Zigzag Paragraph

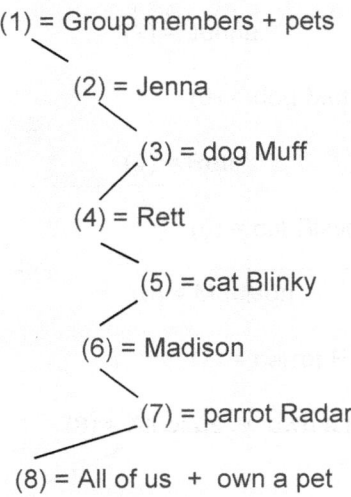

The teacher will give you a list of topics. Choose one and then prepare a zigzag scheme on a piece of notebook paper. Finally, write the paragraph, being sure to include the listing signals (*first, second, third;* or *one, another, another*) and a conclusion that begins with a transition (e.g., *in conclusion, in short*).

PROVERB AND CHREIA

Chapter 5

Introduction

> Blessed is the one who finds wisdom,
>   and the one who gets understanding,
> for the gain from her is better than gain from silver
>   and her profit better than gold.
> She is more precious than jewels,
>   and nothing you desire can compare with her.
> Long life is in her right hand;
>   in her left hand are riches and honor.
> Her ways are ways of pleasantness,
>   and all her paths are peace.
>
>   Proverbs 3:13-17

One of the earliest forms of writing is called wisdom literature. In fact, the very first book ever written, *The Maxims of Ptah-Hotep*, was a collection of wise sayings written down by the Egyptian official Ptah-Hotep in 2500 BC. He wrote down wise sayings to help young people succeed in public service jobs.

In the Old Testament, the book of Proverbs is the wisdom literature of the Hebrew people, and in the New Testament, Paul wrote that Jesus "*became* to us wisdom from God" (1 Cor.

1:30) [emphasis added]. From these examples, we can see that passing on wisdom to the next generation has always been an important part of Biblical living.

Among the ancient teachers, the wisdom of the ages was presented in two forms: the Proverb and the Chreia. Both the Proverb and the Chreia can be about a wise saying, but a Chreia can also be about a wise action.

Because these two elements of the progymnasmata have many similarities, they have been put together in one chapter. As you go through the chapter, you will learn how to present the wisdom of the ancients to your friends, your family members, and even yourself!

THINK IT THROUGH: From your own experiences, can you explain why the following proverbs teach a truth about life?

- Let sleeping dogs lie.

- You can lead a horse to water, but you can't make him drink.

- A penny saved is a penny earned.

Part I: Proverb

Definition and Purpose of Proverb

1. A *proverb* is a short statement that gives advice. It is used to teach moral conduct. However, unlike the Fable, the Proverb simply states the moral without leading up to it with a story.

2. The term *Expanded Proverb* refers to a composition or speech that explores the wisdom of a famous saying. By looking at a saying in multiple ways, we can come to understand it better and have a better chance of applying its truth in our own lives.

3. It is a common purpose of people everywhere to teach their children wisdom. In ancient, medieval, and modern times—in America, Europe, Asia, or Africa—people have the

Teacher's Edition

same basic needs and emotions. Therefore, it is not unusual to find proverbs from different countries that have the same meaning, even though they may state the truth in different words.

 **THINK IT THROUGH:** What seem to be the common teachings about life in these pairs of proverbs?

- **English:** "We all put our pants on one leg at a time."
  Italian: "After the game, the king and the pawn go into the same box."

- **English:** "You can catch more flies with honey than with vinegar."
  Bulgarian: "A gentle word opens an iron gate."

- **English:** "A stitch in time saves nine."
  West African: "Unless you fill up the crack, you will have to build a new wall."

EXERCISE 5.1: Finding Proverbs of Similar Meaning

 <u>Directions</u>: In the exercise below, match the proverbs that have a similar meaning. Place the letter of one proverb in the blank of the matching proverb.

A. **Biblical:** Don't cast pearls before swine (Matthew 7:6).

B. **Chinese:** Enjoy yourself. It's later than you think.

C. **Libyan:** Instruction in youth is like engraving in stone.

D. **English:** The early bird gets the worm.

E. **American:** Stop burning daylight.

F. **Nigerian:** He who is carried on another's back does not appreciate how far off the town is.

_C_ 1. **Biblical:** Train up a child in the way he should go; even when he is old he will not depart from it (Proverb 22:6).

_D_ 2. **German:** Who comes first, eats first.

_A_ 3. **Japanese:** A pig used to dirt turns its nose up at rice.

_F_ 4. **Chinese:** When you eat, remember the farmer.

_B_ 5. **Latin:** *Carpe diem* (seize the day, make most of the day).

_E_ 6. **German:** Lazy bones take all day to get started.

Approaches to Proverb

In this chapter, we will look at seven approaches to the proverb.

Citation	Cite (or quote) the proverb.
Narrative *(if necessary)*	Narrate the basic elements (*who, what, when, where, why, and/or how*) to help the reader understand the proverb better.
Encomium	Praise the wisdom of our ancestors who gave us this observation about human life.
Paraphrase	Put the proverb into your own words.
Example e.g.	Give an example from fact or fiction of another person who made a similar life choice.

Teacher's Edition

Testimony of the Ancients (Corroboration) 	Quote an authority from the past to confirm the wisdom of the action.
Exhortation 	Encourage your readers to make similar life choices.

Model Essay #1: Proverb *without* Narrative

A Proverb about Wishes

Citation + Encomium

It was a wise person who said, "Be careful what you wish for, lest it come true."

Paraphrase

What the proverb means is that sometimes we wish for things without thinking of the consequences. Maybe what we wish for will bring us pain, not gain.

Example

One of the best examples of this proverb is the story of Sejanus, a friend of the emperor Tiberius. Sejanus asked for and received more and more honors and power until he became second only to the emperor himself. But, Sejanus did not realize that along with the honors and powers he was receiving, he was making others jealous. So great did the jealousy grow that, in AD 31, someone accused him of trying to make himself emperor. As a result, Sejanus was tried, sentenced, and put to death—an outcome he certainly had not predicted.

Coin of Tiberius with Sejanus' name on reverse side.

Testimony of the Ancients

But is it wrong for us to wish for things? The apostle John recorded the words of Jesus about wishes: "If you abide in me, and my words abide in you, ask whatever you wish, and it will be done for you" (John 15:7). Notice that this verse does not say that Jesus will give us whatever we want. Instead, there is a condition expressed in the *if-*clause that introduces the statement. It teaches us that when we ask for things that are in accord with those of a person abiding in Him, it will be done. In that case, we are not asking selfishly but within the context of God's plan for us.

Exhortation

All of us wish for things that will improve our lives, but we must always remember to think carefully before expressing our wish. Otherwise, like Sejanus, we might gain one thing but lose another.

EXERCISE 5.2: Analyzing the Proverb about Wishes

Directions: Please answer the questions below, which will help you analyze the model essay above entitled "A Proverb about Wishes."

1. In the first paragraph, underline the proverb that is being discussed and put a squiggly line under the part of the sentence that is "praise."

2. In the Paraphrase, what does the author advise us to do before we make a wish?

   The author advises us to think of the consequences before we make a wish.

3. a. What person is used as an example?

   Sejanus

   b. What did he wish for?

   wealth and power

   c. What unexpected consequences did he receive along with his wish?

   jealousy and death

Teacher's Edition

4. In Testimony of the Ancients:

   (a) What Bible verse is quoted as support? *John 15:7*

   (b) Underline the part of the verse that is intended to help us with our wishes.

Model Essay #2: Proverb *with* Narrative

A Proverb about Thrift

Citation + Praise

<u>It was a wise person who said, "Waste not, want not."</u>

Paraphrase

This proverb means that we should be thrifty, not wasteful.

Narrative

The meaning of the verb *to want* has changed over the years. Nowadays, it means about the same thing as *to desire*, but it originally meant *to lack*. Most of us know about Charles Dickens' famous novel *A Christmas Carol*. In that story, the Ghost of Christmas Past opens the folds of his coat to reveal two starving children named Ignorance and *Want*. They represent the poor of the world who lack food and other necessities of life. Thus, to *want* something originally meant to *lack* it. This is the meaning of the word *want* in the proverb, "Waste not, want not."

Example

One of the best examples of the wisdom of the saying "Waste not, want not" is the narrative of the Prodigal Son from Luke 15. In that story, a young man demanded his inheritance from his father while his father was still alive. Shortly after receiving it, he "gathered all he had and took a journey into a far country, and there he squandered his property in reckless living" (v. 13). Soon a famine came on the land, and the young man had no money with which to buy the things he needed. So great was his hunger that he ended up begging to be fed the pigs' food. Fortunately, he repented of his sin and returned home. His father welcomed him back, but if the young man had exercised wisdom, he would never have placed himself in such a horrible position to begin with.

Exhortation

It is easy to waste money and other resources when we think only about the present moment. However, the proverb "Waste not, want not" teaches us in four short words a great lesson of life: <u>use your money and supplies wisely so that in a time of need you will not find yourself in want.</u>

EXERCISE 5.3: Analyzing the Proverb about Thrift

<u>Directions</u>: Please answer the questions below, which will help you analyze the model essay above entitled "A Proverb about Thrift."

1. In the first paragraph, <u>underline</u> the proverb that is being discussed and put squiggly lines under the part of the sentence that is "praise."

2. In the Paraphrase, the point of the proverb is that we should be *thrifty*,

   not *wasteful*.

3. a. The purpose of the Narrative is to explain a verb from the quotation. Which verb is it? *To want*

   b. Since Narrative is not always necessary, why do you think it the author thought it was necessary here?

   It is necessary to explain the original meaning of the word "want" because otherwise readers might misunderstand the meaning of the proverb.

4. What example from the Bible is used to explain the proverb?

   The story of the prodigal son from Luke 15

5. The key part of the Exhortation appears in the last sentence of the essay. Underline the part that follows the colon (:).

Finding Proverbs and "Testimony of the Ancients"

You may have expressed an opinion in the past and some wag responded by saying, "Oh, yeah? Who says?" From a remark like this, we can see that a listener naturally seeks authority for what a speaker says.

Plato and Aristotle

This is why teachers from the earliest times have encouraged students to find support from a respected person. They called this technique "testimony of the ancients." Yes, it may be true that you think your teacher or parent is ancient, but the idea here is to choose the thoughts of someone who lived in the past and whose words have stood the test of time.

But how does a person go about finding who said what in the long ago? There are actually several resources that can help. The next three exercises will direct you to several of them and provide you with some practice using them.

EXERCISE 5.4: Finding Testimony of the Ancients on the Internet

Directions: Please complete the exercises below, which will assist you in the skill of finding proverbs and wise sayings on the Internet.

1. **Classical World:**
   a. On the Internet, go to the web site for *World of Quotes* at <www.worldofquotes.com>.
   b. In the left column of the home page, scroll down to Popular Proverb Origins, where you will see a list of nationalities.
   c. Click on "Greek."
   d. When the Greek proverbs appear, find one that you like and copy it in this space.
      Greek Proverb: *Selections will vary.*

2. **Your Ancestry:**
    a. Go back to the home page for *World of Quotes*.
    b. Scroll down to the Popular Proverb Origins list again.
    c. This time, click on "More Proverbs." A longer list of nationalities appears.
    d. From this list, choose your own ethnic heritage. For example, if your ancestors came from Scotland, you would click "Scotland." You can search by either your father's or mother's heritage—or both.
    e. Skim the proverbs until you find one that you like and copy it in the space below.

    Nationality: *Selections will vary.*

    Proverb: *Selections will vary.*

3. **Bible:**
    a. Go to the *Topical Bible* web site at <www.openbible.info/topics>.
    b. In the search bar, type a topic such as Anger, Jealousy, or Friendship.
    c. Click Search.
    d. Skim the verses that appear and choose one that you like.
    e. Write the chosen verse in the space below. Be sure to give the verse reference (such as John 3:16).

    Topic: *Selections will vary.*

    Verse: *Selections will vary.*

    Reference: *Selections will vary.*

4. **Bible:**
    a. Go to the Bible Gateway web site at <www.biblegateway.com>.
    b. Choose English Standard Version (ESV) for your search.
    c. Imagine that you have memorized a verse from the ESV, and you remember that it contains the phrase, *by a single offering.*
    d. Enter *by a single offering* in the search bar. Then in the space below, copy the entire verse and the reference.

Teacher's Edition

Verse: *For by a single offering he has perfected for all time those who are being sanctified.*

Reference: *Hebrews 10:14*

EXERCISE 5.5: Paraphrasing Proverbs

Directions: Please complete the exercises below, which will assist you in the skill of paraphrasing proverbs.

1. Benjamin Franklin is very famous for his many wise sayings, some of which raise a little chuckle. For example, he once said, "Fish and visitors smell in three days." If Dennis the Menace ever came for a long stay at your house, you might get a feeling for what ol' Ben meant!

   a. In the search bar of your web browser, enter the following Internet address: <www.benandverse.com/poorben/index.shtml>.

   b. Here you will find a topical index for Franklin's proverbs. Choose a topic that interests you and click on it.

   c. Now you will see two columns. In the first column is Ben Franklin's proverb in the language of his day. In the right column is a modern paraphrase in verse form. Find a proverb and paraphrase that you like and copy them in the following space:

   Proverb: *Selections will vary.*

   Verse (Paraphrase): *Selections will vary.*

2. Below are three Bible verses which can be paraphrased using, "If…then…." Use the prompts to help you paraphrase the verses. The first one serves as an example.

   a. "A joyful heart is a good medicine" (Proverbs 17:22a).

If you __are happy__, then you will __feel good__

b. "A soft answer turns away wrath" (Proverbs 15:1a).

If you __speak in a kind way__, then you will __be able to prevent an argument__

c. "A fool's lips walk into a fight" (Proverbs 18:6a)

If you __"lip off" to people__,

then you will __find yourself in a fight.__

Quills #1: Proverb

Your teacher will give you the instructions you need to write an Expanded Proverb.

Part II: Chreia

Most Americans know that our sixteenth president, Abraham Lincoln, was known as "Honest Abe." There is a narrative that explains how he came by that name. It goes this way:

> Abe Lincoln could not endure the thought of cheating anyone, even though it had been done unintentionally. One day a woman bought a bill of goods in Offutt's store, where Abe was working, amounting to something over two dollars. She paid Abe the money and went away satisfied. That night, on going over the sales of the day, Abe found that he had charged the woman six and one-fourth cents too much. After closing the store, though it was late, he could not go home to supper or to bed till he had restored that sixpence to its proper owner. She lived more than two miles away, but that did not matter to Abe Lincoln. When he had returned the money to the astonished woman, he walked back to the village with a long step and a light heart, content with doing his duty.[20]

This short narrative is called a Chreia. In this section, you will learn its definition, purpose, and techniques.

Definition and Purpose of Chreia

As shown in the first part of the chapter, proverbs and wise sayings can inspire and guide people. But at the same time, we are also aware of the Biblical statement, "But be *doers* of the word, and not hearers only. . ." (James 1:22).

The rhetoric teachers in the ancient world also understood this link, and so they created a companion exercise to the Proverb. It is called by the Greek word *Chreia* (pronounced KRAY-uh), which means *anecdote*. According to the Merriam-Webster dictionary, an anecdote is usually a "short narrative of an interesting, amusing, or biographical incident."[21] In other words, a *Chreia* explores the behavior of a wise or a foolish person so that readers or listeners can learn from the experience of others.

The anecdote about Abraham Lincoln returning six and one-fourth cents teaches us a valuable life lesson about honesty. That is the purpose of the Chreia.

 **THINK IT THROUGH:** With your classmates, consider these famous anecdotes. What life lesson does each one teach?

- The Biblical anecdote about the widow's mite (Luke 21:1-4).
- The brief Biblical narrative about what Paul and Silas did when an earthquake brought down the jail where they were imprisoned (Acts 16:25-34).

Approaches to the Chreia

As with the Proverb, a fully expanded Chreia has nine approaches. In this chapter, we will again look at seven of them. They are quite similar to the approaches to Proverb but are somewhat different based on the fact that the Proverb is related to a person's words, while a Chreia is related to a person's actions.

Narrative + Citation	Narrate the anecdote. If the anecdote includes a key quotation, include (cite) the quotation as well.
Encomium	Praise the person who chose the wise course of action.
Explanation	Explain what the person's action teaches us.
Example	Give an example from fact or fiction of another person who made a similar life choice.
Testimony of the Ancients (Corroboration)	Quote an authority from the past to confirm the wisdom of the action.

Exhortation 	Encourage your readers to make similar life choices.

Model Chreia

NOTE: In the opening paragraph of the model chreia, there are four Greek names. Their pronunciation is as follows:

Sophocles: SOF-ə-kleez *Creon: KREE-on*

Antigone: an-TIG-ə-nee *Polyneices: POL-ee-NĪS-eez*

The Courage of Antigone

Narration + Citation

In about 441 BC, the Greek playwright Sophocles wrote a play called *Antigone*. This play is about a young woman who disobeyed an evil ruler, King Creon. In a recent battle against the king, one of her brothers had fought for the king, but her brother Polyneices had been killed in rebellion against the king. As a result of Polyneices' rebellion, King Creon would not allow anyone to bury Polyneices' body. He preferred that wolves devour the body as a warning to others not to rebel. However, Antigone could not tolerate this inhumanity against her brother, and she buried him in defiance of Creon's order. At her trial (in Scene 4 of the play), Creon argued that she should not treat the rebel brother the same as the loyal brother, who had died fighting for Creon. But Antigone replied, "'Tis not my nature to join in hating, but in loving."[22] As a result, Antigone was put to death at the king's command.

Encomium

The author Sophocles showed great wisdom when he wrote this brave assertion for Antigone. He is to be praised for understanding the importance of honoring one's family.

Explanation

In this play, Sophocles is trying to say that loving is better than hating. <u>We should conduct ourselves in such a way that our conscience is clear. We must stand up for what is right.</u>

Example

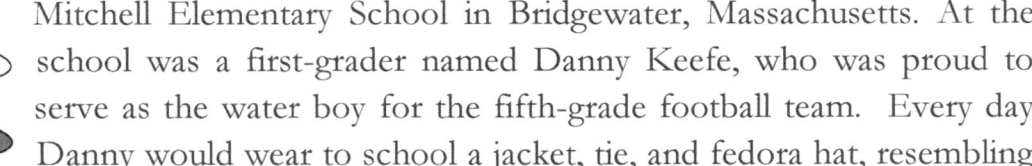

A modern-day example of this truth occurred in the fall of 2013 at Mitchell Elementary School in Bridgewater, Massachusetts. At the school was a first-grader named Danny Keefe, who was proud to serve as the water boy for the fifth-grade football team. Every day Danny would wear to school a jacket, tie, and fedora hat, resembling perhaps the legendary football coach Bear Bryant. No one loved the team more than Danny, and the team members appreciated his support.

Now, six years earlier, Danny had been born prematurely, and bleeding in his brain had left him with a speech disorder as he grew up. The way he talked—along with his jacket, tie, and hat—made him a little "different" from the other kids, so local bullies began picking on Danny. They would taunt him by saying, "Why don't you just talk!" They would even yank his hat off and rub mulch in his hair.

When the quarterback of the football team, a fifth-grader named Tommy Cooney, found out about this, he decided that the players needed to put a stop to the bullying. So, on November 20, all forty-five members of the team wore jackets and ties to school to show their support for Danny. When asked by news reporters why he organized this show of support, Tommy Cooney replied, "We thought we would all come to school like Danny and sponsor Danny to show Danny that we love him – that we love him very much."[23]

Fortunately, in our country, the boys at Mitchell Elementary had a better result than Antigone did in Creon's kingdom. The government, in the form of the Massachusetts House of Representatives, honored Danny and his "band of brothers" with a special citation and a banquet for showing that, like Antigone, their nature was not to join in hating, but in loving.

Teacher's Edition

Testimony of the Ancients

The apostle John, referring to Christians as "the children of God," spoke plainly about this subject when he wrote, <u>"Little children, let us not love in word or talk but in deed and in truth" (I John 3:18).</u> Our love for others is to be shown in our actions.

Exhortation

As you go through life, you may well find yourself in a situation where you will need to stand up for another person. Always remember these teachings and find ways to <u>show God's love in your deeds.</u>

EXERCISE 5.6: Analyzing a Chreia

 <u>Directions</u>: Analyze "The Courage of Antigone" by answering the following questions.

1. Paragraph 1 (Narration + Citation):

   a. From which play does the anecdote come?

   Antigone

   b. What did Antigone do, knowing that the punishment was death?

   She buried the body of her rebel brother.

   c. What did Antigone say about her action?

   "'Tis not my nature to join in __*hating*__, but in __*loving*__."

2. In Paragraph 2 (Encomium), who is praised for his wisdom?

   The playwright Sophocles

3. In Paragraph 3 (Paraphrase), underline the paraphrase of what Antigone said.

4. Briefly summarize the Example that is given in Paragraph 4.

   A first-grader was being picked on, so the fifth-grade football players stood up for him.

Proverb and Chreia | 79

5. In Paragraph 5 (Testimony of the Ancients), underline the Bible verse that is quoted.

6. In order to emphasize the main point, the author has put the key phrase of Paragraph 6 (Exhortation) near the end of the last sentence. Underline the key words.

Quills #2: Chreia

Your teacher will give you the instructions you need to write a Chreia.

ENCOMIUM AND INVECTIVE

Chapter 6

To the Church in Pergamum

¹²"And to the angel of the church in Pergamum write: 'The words of him who has the sharp two-edged sword.

Sketched 19th-century Reconstruction of Pergamum

¹³"'I know where you dwell, where Satan's throne is. Yet you hold fast my name, and you did not deny my faith even in the days of Antipas my faithful witness, who was killed among you, where Satan dwells. ¹⁴But I have a few things against you: you have some there who hold the teaching of Balaam, who taught Balak to put a stumbling block before the sons of Israel, so that they might eat food sacrificed to idols and practice sexual immorality. ¹⁵So also you have some who hold the teaching of the Nicolaitans. ¹⁶Therefore repent. If not, I will come to you soon and war against them with the sword of my mouth. ¹⁷He who has an ear, let him hear what the Spirit says to the churches. To the one who conquers I will give some of the hidden manna, and I will give him a white stone, with a new name written on the stone that no one knows except the one who receives it.'"

Revelation 2:12-17

This passage from the book of Revelation in the Bible contains two parts. Verse 13 contains *praise* for the church in Pergamum, while Verses 14-17 contain *blame*. In other words, this passage of Scripture from the New Testament combines two elements of the progymnasmata: Encomium (praise) and Invective (blame). The purpose of this chapter is to explain these two elements and give you a chance to practice them.

Definitions and Purposes of Encomium and Invective

- An *encomium* is a composition or a speech whose purpose is offer praise.

- An *invective* is a composition or a speech whose purpose is to offer blame.

THINK IT THROUGH: From your study of history, what people do you consider worthy to receive a composition or speech of praise? Why?

THINK IT THROUGH: From your study of history, what people do you think deserve public criticism (or blame)?

Subjects and Occasions of Encomium and Invective

In our day and age, we still use Encomium and Invective. Some examples are listed below.

Occasions for Encomium (Praise)

- Funerals

- Wedding receptions

- Nominations for political office

- Awards ceremonies

- Retirement parties

Teacher's Edition

Occasions for Invective (Blame)

- Commentary in the media about an evil-doer (e.g., tyrant, assassin, terrorist)

- Sermons about Biblical figures or groups who committed evil

- Speech to a jury about a murderer who deserves punishment

 **THINK IT THROUGH:**

- Tell the class about a time you heard someone praise another person publicly.

- Tell the class about a time you heard someone criticize another person publicly.

Approaches to Encomium and Invective

Full-length Encomia and Invectives have five approaches. In this chapter, we will focus on three: background, character (virtues or vices), and deeds (good or evil).

Approach	Explanation
Background + Narrative	Introduce the person by telling his/her parents, place of birth, education, and other things that help us understand the person.
Character	**In Encomium:** Tell the person's *virtues*: loyalty, faith, fair-mindedness, helpfulness, etc. **In Invective:** Tell the person's *vices*: drug-addiction, cruelty, injustice, double-dealing, anger, etc.

Encomium and Invective | 83

Deeds	**In Encomium:** Tell the person's specific achievements: heroic acts, exploration, discovery, awards, etc.
	In Invective: Tell the person's specific evil deeds: treachery, murder, acts of cruelty, bullying, robbery, etc.

Part I: Encomium

EXERCISE 6.1: Distinguishing between Traits and Deeds

Directions: Below are some examples of encomium-like statements from modern times. Read each one and determine whether the statement refers to a good character trait or a good deed. Place the letter of the correct answer in the corresponding blank.

A. Good character traits
B. Good deeds

__B__ 1. *In May 1940, the Nazis invaded the Netherlands. At that time, Casper ten Boom (b. 1859) owned a watchmaker's shop in Amsterdam.*

Encomium: "In 1940 when the Nazis required all Jews in the Netherlands to wear a yellow star, Casper, though not a Jew himself, stood in line to obtain a star, which he proudly wore. The ten Boom family smuggled in bricks and mortar in order to construct a small room, 2 feet x 7 feet, accessible through a small closet in [daughter] Corrie's bedroom located on the top floor of the house. A bell was installed to warn 'guests' when anyone suspicious approached the house"[24] (David R. Barnhart).

Teacher's Edition

___B___ 2. *Mother Teresa of Calcutta (1910-1997) was a Roman Catholic nun from Albania. She spent most of her life as a missionary in India.*

Encomium: "In 1952 the first Home for the Dying was opened in space made available by the City of Calcutta [India]. Over the years, Mother Teresa's Missionaries of Charity grew from 12 to thousands serving the 'poorest of the poor' in 450 centers around the world. Mother Teresa created many homes for the dying and the unwanted from Calcutta to New York to Albania. She was one of the pioneers of establishing homes for AIDS victims"[25] (EWTN).

___A___ 3. *Sir Winston Churchill (1874-1965) was the British Prime Minister from 1940 to 1945, the years of World War II, and again from 1950 to 1955. When Churchill passed away, Dwight D. Eisenhower, American general during World War II and the thirty-fourth president of the United States, spoke at the funeral.*

Encomium: "To those men [Americans and British who fought in World War II] Winston Churchill was Britain—he was the embodiment of British defiance to threat, her courage in adversity, her calmness in danger, her moderation in success. Among the allies, his name was spoken with respect, admiration, and affection. Although they loved to chuckle at his foibles, they knew he was a staunch friend. They felt his inspirational leadership. They counted him a fighter in their ranks"[26] (Dwight D. Eisenhower).

Organization: Writing a Conclusion

Just as a stand-alone paragraph needs a brief concluding sentence, an essay needs a brief concluding paragraph. In this chapter, you will have the opportunity to examine and practice two popular techniques for writing a conclusion.

The first technique is summary. The second is quotation. It is even possible to use both techniques and still have a paragraph of only two sentences. As you read the model Encomium and the model Invective, you will have a chance to look more closely at techniques for conclusions.

Model Encomium

A Tribute to Fanny Crosby

Background + Narrative

Frances Jane Crosby, better known as Fanny Crosby, was born in 1820 in Brooklyn, New York. Her parents were missionaries. When Fanny was only six weeks old, she developed an eye infection. She was treated by a man who claimed to be a doctor but was not, and his bad treatment caused her to lose her vision. She remained blind until her death at age 94. Fanny loved music and poetry, and even as a child composed hymns. In adulthood, she became a well-known hymn writer as well as a teacher and a worker in a rescue mission.

Character

Fanny Crosby had many admirable character traits. First, she was an optimistic person. Instead of being filled with hatred and resentment about her situation, she went on to receive an education and even as a youth read a poem before Congress advocating more schools to educate the blind. Second, she was a devout Christian. She told people that her blindness on this earth only meant that, after death, the first face she would ever see would be that of her Savior.

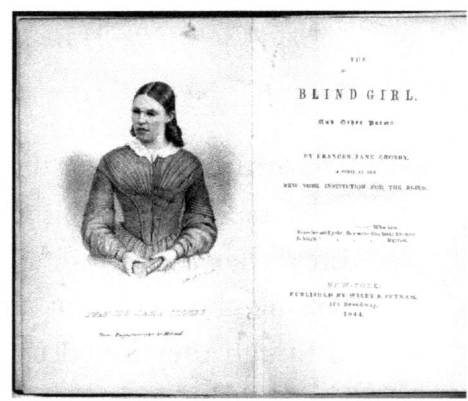

Frontispiece of *A Blind Girl* (a collection of poems by Fanny Crosby)

Achievements

Over her lifetime, Fanny Crosby wrote more than 8,000 hymns and gospel songs that became standard in churches throughout the United States. Some examples are "Victory in Jesus," "Blessed Assurance," and "Pass Me Not, O Gentle Savior." Hip-hop singer M. C. Hammer even took the latter and recorded it in his own style as "Do Not Pass Me By" in 1991. Fanny also wrote some patriotic songs and four books of poems as well as an inspirational autobiography. Then, as praise songs emerged in the late twentieth-century, some of Fanny's hymns continued in popularity and are now familiar to a new generation in the twenty-first century. Some examples are "Praise Him, Praise Him" and "To God Be the Glory."

Teacher's Edition

Conclusion

In conclusion, Fanny Crosby was one of the most prolific and beloved hymn writers in history. Even though she could not see, she made it easy for millions of people to see Christ through her songs. Her simple headstone bears the humble phrase, "She did what she could," but what she did was wonderful indeed.

EXERCISE 6.2: Examining an Encomium

Directions: Analyze essay entitled "A Tribute to Fanny Crosby" by answering the questions below.

1. What do we learn about Fanny Crosby in Background?

   a. Parents: _missionaries_

   b. Place of birth: _Brooklyn, NY_

   c. Year of birth: _1820_

   d. What happened when she was an infant: _She lost her vision_

2. What two character traits (virtues) are given in Character?

   a. _optimism_   b. _devout Christian_

3. Answer these questions about the section called Achievements.

   a. Music: Fanny wrote both _hymns_ and _gospel_ songs as well as _patriotic_ songs.

   b. Writing: Fanny wrote _poems_ and an _autobiography_.

4. Which of these is the main idea of Achievements?

   A. M. C. Hammer recorded a version of one hymn in 1991.

   B. <u>Fanny's songs have remained popular for several generations.</u>

   C. Some of Fanny's songs are now considered praise songs.

Encomium and Invective | 87

5. Regarding the Conclusion:

   a. One of the techniques for a conclusion is summary. Which of Fanny's achievements is reviewed in the conclusion? *Fanny's achievement as a hymn writer*

   b. Another technique for a conclusion is a quotation. What is the quotation and where does it come from?

   "She did what she could," a quote from her headstone.

   c. Since the Conclusion is a finishing touch, you might think of it as a bow you attach to a birthday present you have wrapped. Just as the bow does not remain loose on the package but is attached with tape, so the quotation cannot just be stuck into the paragraph. It needs "tape"—which, in this case, will be some kind of comment that attaches it to the rest of the paragraph. What comment was added after the quotation in the essay about Fanny Crosby?

   What she did was wonderful indeed!

Quills #1: Encomium

 Your teacher will give you the instructions you need to write an Encomium.

Teacher's Edition

Part II: Invective

EXERCISE 6.3: Distinguishing between Traits and Deeds

<u>Directions</u>: Below are some examples of invective statements in today's media. Read each one and determine whether the statement refers to bad character traits or bad deeds. Place the letter of the correct answer in the corresponding blank.

A. Bad character traits
B. Bad deeds

__B__ 1. *In the wake of the 9/11 attack on the World Trade Center in New York in 2001, the fire fighters of New York (FDNY) labored to remove human remains from the debris. Two months later, the mayor of New York, Rudy Giuliani, ordered them to cease the search for remains and bulldoze the area, which the firefighters considered an insult. In 2008, the fire fighters' union refused to invite Giuliani to an FDNY-sponsored debate of presidential candidate, saying:*

FDNY Fire Fighter at World Trade Center

Invective: "Mayor Giuliani's actions meant that the fire fighters and citizens who perished would either remain buried at Ground Zero forever, with no closure for families, or be removed like garbage and deposited at the Fresh Kills Landfill"[27] (Harold A. Shaitberger).

__A__ 2. *In 1994, Aldrich Ames, an officer in the Central Intelligence Agency (CIA), was sent to prison for treason against the United States. As a result of his treason, many people gathering information for the United State were killed.*

Invective: Ames "is an extremely despicable human being who did this so he could have a nicer house and a Jaguar automobile"[28] (R. James Woolsey, Director of the CIA).

Aldrich Ames

__A__ 3. *In 1919, the sports world was rocked by the Black Sox Scandal, when eight members of the Chicago White Sox team were accused of throwing the World Series to the Cincinnati Reds. Specifically, they were accused of teaming up with gamblers to receive money for intentionally losing the games. They were banned from baseball for life. However, many say the players were in*

Encomium and Invective | 89

desperate financial straits because of the White Sox owner, Charles Comiskey. Below is a law student's criticism of Comiskey.

Invective: "By any measure, Comiskey was a tightwad. . . . In 1918, attendance at baseball games across the country dropped because of World War I. Owners cut players' salaries the next year as a result. When attendance in Chicago actually went up, Comiskey refused to bring salaries back to their previous level. While most teams gave their players $4 a day for meals, Comiskey would pay only $3. The White Sox had the filthiest uniforms in the league because Comiskey wanted to cut laundry bills. Comiskey had some of the best players in the country on his team, but paid them all far below what players of comparable talent were earning elsewhere"[29] (Traci Peterson, University of Missouri at Kansas City).

Charles Comiskey

Model Invective

An Invective against King Saul

Background + Narrative

Saul was the first king of Israel. The people had demanded that God give them a king, and though God warned them they would rue the day they took a king, they insisted that they wanted to be like other nations and needed a king. God gave them Saul. As God had foretold, Saul's kingship brought disaster on Israel.

Vices

Saul had three great vices. First, he was very jealous. In particular, he was jealous of David, whom the Lord had chosen to replace him. Secondly, he was disobedient to the Lord. The Lord asked Saul for total obedience, but Saul gave only partial obedience. This disobedience led to his third vice: his murderous heart. Because Saul was disobedient, the Lord withdrew his own Spirit from Saul and put in its place an evil spirit to torment him. Soon after, we see a third vice: Saul flew into murderous rages.

Evil Deeds

Because of his jealousy and his evil spirit, Saul committed evil deeds. He set out to kill David, who had saved Israel from the Philistines by killing Goliath and who had done Saul no wrong. Then, when Saul's son Jonathan, David's friend, tried to soften his father's heart, Saul heaved his spear at him in anger. In the end, this murderous rage was poured out on himself. As the Philistines prepared to attack, Saul was still not willing to repent and trust the Lord. Instead, deciding he would rather kill himself than be captured, he fell on his own sword.

*Death of Saul
By Gustave Doré*

Conclusion

Saul, the first king of Israel, was a sinful man. He was jealous and disobedient. He was given over to an evil spirit and, in the end, had not victory, but death.

EXERCISE 6.4: Analyzing an Invective

<u>Directions</u>: Analyze the essay entitled "An Invective against Saul" by answering the questions below.

1. In Background + Narrative:

   a. Saul is identified as a <u>king</u> of <u>Israel</u>.

   b. How did it come to pass that God gave Israel a king?

   The Israelites wanted a king so that they could be like other nations.

3. In Character, what three bad character traits (vices) are named?

   a. *jealousy (esp. of David)*

   b. *disobedience toward God*

   c. *murderous rages*

4. In Evil Deeds, what three evil deeds are mentioned?

   a. <u>attempt to kill David</u>

   b. <u>throwing a spear at his own son</u>

   c. <u>killing himself instead of trusting God</u>

5. What type of conclusion is used?

   A. <u>Summary</u>

   B. Quote + comment

   C. Both A and B

Quills #2: Invective

 Your teacher will give you the instructions you need to write an Invective.

REFUTATION AND CONFIRMATION

Chapter 7

Introduction

The Adventures of Pinocchio (1883) by the Italian author Carlo Collodi tells the story of a poor woodcarver named Gepetto, who carves a marionette from a special block of wood and names him Pinocchio, which means "pine eye." Treating Pinocchio as his own son, Gepetto sends the "boy" to school, but on the way, Pinocchio sells a schoolbook in order to buy a theater ticket. One bad decision leads to another until Pinocchio finds himself with five gold coins (intended for his father) and a predicament from which he is rescued by a Fairy. In Chapter 17, we see Pinocchio's greed get the better of him. It begins when the Fairy starts asking him questions:

"Where are the gold pieces now?" the Fairy asked.

"I lost them," answered Pinocchio, but he told a lie, for he had them in his pocket.

As he spoke, his nose, long though it was, became at least two inches longer.

"And where did you lose them?"

"In the wood near by."

At this second lie, his nose grew a few more inches.

"If you lost them in the near-by wood," said the Fairy, "we'll look for them and find them, for everything that is lost there is always found."

"Ah, now I remember," replied the Marionette, becoming more and more confused. "I did not lose the gold pieces, but I swallowed them when I drank the medicine." At this third lie, his nose became longer than ever, so long that he could not even turn around. If he turned to the right, he knocked it against the bed or into the windowpanes; if he turned to the left, he struck the walls or the door; if he raised it a bit, he almost put the Fairy's eyes out.

The Fairy sat looking at him and laughing.

"Why do you laugh?" the Marionette asked her, worried now at the sight of his growing nose.

"I am laughing at your lies."

"How do you know I am lying?"

"Lies, my boy, are known in a moment. There are two kinds of lies, lies with short legs and lies with long noses. Yours, just now, happen to have long noses."

Pinocchio, not knowing where to hide his shame, tried to escape from the room, but his nose had become so long that he could not get it out of the door.

Don't you wish that it was always so easy to determine when a person is lying? Unfortunately, in the real world, it is much more difficult to determine whether someone is telling the truth or not. In order to establish the truth of a matter in a court of law, lawyers,  in their training, use time-tested methods that help determine the truth. One of the main purposes of a classical education is to prepare citizens for life in a republic, and since courtrooms are very much a part of a democracy, it is not surprising that students in ancient times were given skills to help them become "truth detectors." The purpose of this chapter is to introduce you to those skills and give you an opportunity to practice them.

Definition and Purpose

1. To refute something is to prove that it is not true. The process is called Refutation.

2. To confirm something is to prove that it *is* true. The process is called Confirmation.

3. The purpose of Refutation is to point out weaknesses in a person's narrative of events.

4. The purpose of Confirmation is to point out the strengths in a person's narrative.

 **THINK IT THROUGH:**

- Narrate for your classmates a time when you were fairly certain someone was not telling the truth. What made you suspicious?

- Narrate a time when you were certain someone was innocent and were able to come to his or her defense.

Approaches to Refutation and Confirmation

When trying to prove or disprove the truth of a narrative, there are four basic questions you can ask:

Is the narrative:

- possible or impossible?
- probable or improbable?
- clear or unclear?
- consistent or inconsistent?

The chart below provides explanations and examples for these four approaches.

Possible or Impossible?
Here you want to ask if the event is possible according to the laws of nature.

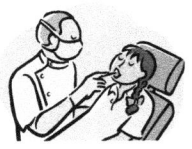

Example: If Agatha was at the dentist's office when something was stolen from her classmate's locker, Agatha could not have been the thief because it would be impossible for her to be in two places at the same time.

Probable or Improbable?
Here you want to ask if the events are too unusual to have happened. In other words, did the event *probably* happen in the way it was described?

Example: Since we cannot be 100% sure if there is life on other planets, we might conclude it is *possible* that space aliens landed in New Mexico, but such an event would certainly be very unusual. Many people would argue that it *probably* did not happen. In other words, the narrative is improbable.

Clear or Unclear?
Here you want to determine whether the facts of the case are clear or not.

Example: If Charlie reports that somebody beat him up but cannot tell the police when or where the attack happened, then obviously the facts are not clear. This might lead police to believe the narrative is not true.

Teacher's Edition

> **Consistent or Inconsistent?**
>
> Here you want to find out if there are any contradictions in the story.

Example: Suppose while the Millers are on vacation, Gillie is being paid to water their plants. When they arrive home, the plants have all died. Gillie, however, says that he watered the plants every day. Then later he says he watered them on Monday and Wednesday. Then later he says he watered them on Thursday. Since the story keeps changing, the neighbors might suspect Gillie is not telling the truth. His story is inconsistent.

EXERCISE 7.1: Truth-Detecting

Below are some narratives of criminal cases that have made the news. Using the above chart to guide you, determine with your classmates whether you think the narrative would be easier for police to refute or to confirm.

1. In a Midwestern city, a fellow we'll call Chuck was unable to pay his attorney, so he decided the quickest way to get the money was to rob someone. He decided to rob his employer, whom we'll call Mr. Dart. Mr. Dart, who had many employees, did not know Chuck personally and would not recognize him—or so Chuck thought. He spent a few evenings casing Dart's home, not realizing that on one of these evenings he accidentally kicked a small bag of trash fell out  of his car. Thinking all was well with his plan, Chuck waited for Mr. Dart to leave for work, pulled a gun on him, and hopped into the back seat of Dart's car. He then ordered Dart to drive to an ATM machine. Chuck kept referring to the employer as "Mr. Dart," so Dart figured that somehow this fellow knew him. At a stoplight, Dart was able to bail out of the car, and Chuck hopped into the front seat and drove off. When the police found the car on a dirt road near Dart's home, they noticed nearby tire tracks and made casts of them. Before the police left, Dart recalled the strange bag of trash that had shown up on his driveway. Upon opening that bag, the police found envelopes that clearly displayed Chuck's address. The police were able to arrest Chuck, who was then

identified as an employee of Dart's company and whose tires matched those found at the scene. What do you make of the elements of this narrative?

a. To the police, would it seem possible or impossible Chuck was the robber? Explain your answer.

Possible: The robber knew Mr. Dart's name.

b. Would it seem probable or improbable that Chuck was the robber? Explain your answer.

Probable: Chuck's name was in the trash found on Mr. Dart's driveway.

c. Would it seem clear or unclear that Chuck was the robber? Explain your answer.

Clear: The tire tracks where the robber made his getaway matched those of the casts the police made.

2. In 1980, an Australian couple, Lindy and Michael Chamberlain, were camping in the Outback with their 9-week-old baby girl named Azaria and her two older brothers. Toward evening, Mr. and Mrs. Chamberlain were preparing dinner nearby the tent, where the baby girl was sleeping. Suddenly they heard the baby cry out. Mrs. Chamberlain dashed into the tent only to see a dingo slinking out of the tent. The baby was missing from her bassinet. Police were able to find the baby's jumpsuit but not the jacket she had been wearing. They claimed there was a bloody handprint on the jumpsuit. Mr. Chamberlain explained the disappearance in the same way as Mrs. Chamberlain, and fellow campers said they also heard a low animal growl and a baby's cry. However, two years later the mother received a life sentence for the baby's murder. What do you make of the mother and father's narrative?

a. Is it possible or impossible that a dingo could carry off a 10-pound baby?

It is possible for a dingo to carry off a 10-pound baby. It is big enough to do so

Teacher's Edition

b. Is it probable or improbable that a dingo would enter a tent with adult humans nearby?

Answers will vary, but it may seem improbable that a dingo would enter a tent when humans were nearby. It might smell humans and be fearful.

c. Is it clear or unclear that the handprint on the jumpsuit was bloody?

From the facts given, it is not clear that the handprint on the jumpsuit was bloody.

d. Were the statements of the parents and the fellow campers consistent or inconsistent? (That is, were there any conflicting statements?)

All the narratives were consistent.

3. In the Australian case, four years after the mother went to prison, an Englishman disappeared while hiking in the same area. When his body was discovered, the investigation proved that he had fallen off a cliff and had landed in a "dingo lair," where he died. While examining the lair, police discovered among the brush a remnant of the jacket which had never been recovered in the 1980 case. In addition, tests proved that the handprint on the baby's clothing was not made by blood, but by the red soil of the Outback area. What do you make of these new elements to the narrative?

   a. Do the new elements make the parents' narrative more possible or more impossible to believe? *The new elements make it more possible to believe the parents' narrative.*

   b. Do the new elements make it more probable or less probable that a dingo took the baby?

   The details make it more probable that a dingo took the baby.

   c. Do the new elements make the nature of the handprint more clear or more unclear?

   The new elements make the presence of dingos in the area more clear.

   d. Are the new elements consistent or inconsistent with the parents' narrative?

   The new elements are consistent with the parents' narrative.

4. On August 4, 2014, in a NASCAR race in New York, one of the drivers, Tony Stewart, sent another driver, Kevin Ward, Jr., into the wall during one of the laps around the racetrack. Very angry about what had happened, Kevin Ward got out of  his car, and NASCAR officers waved the yellow caution flag, which requires drivers to slow their cars. When Stewart's car came round, Ward stepped into the track to confront him and was hit by the right rear wheel on Stewart's car. He was killed on impact. Two videos of the race showed the entire incident. Ward's family argued that Stewart had not slowed his car, as he should have, when the track was under caution. The video showed Ward stepping into the track but did not show Stewart swerving toward him. Blood tests showed that Ward, the man who was killed, was under the influence of marijuana at the time of the incident. Stewart stated that he did not intentionally hit Ward. Prosecutors gave the case to a grand jury, who had to decide whether to take Stewart's case before a judge and jury. The various conclusions they could have reached were:

- manslaughter in the second degree (meaning Ward's death was caused by Stewart's recklessness).

- criminally negligent homicide (meaning Stewart deliberately killed Ward).

- accident (meaning Stewart would not be charged with a crime).

What would you say about the following matters?

   a. Is it possible or impossible to know if Stewart intentionally killed Ward?

   Answers will vary, but it is not possible to know what is in another person's mind.

   b. Is it probable or improbable that Ward's use of marijuana was a factor in this tragedy?

   Answers will vary, but it is probable to argue that marijuana impaired Ward's judgment.

   c. Is it clear or unclear that Stewart's car swerved toward Ward?

   It is clear from the video that he did not swerve.

   d. Are Stewart's statements consistent with the video?

   Stewart says he did not hit Ward intentionally, and the video shows that he did not swerve. This suggests consistency.

   e. Based on your analysis, do you think the grand jury brought Stewart to trial or not?

   Answers will vary, but in reality, the grand jury did not find enough evidence to indict Stewart.

Organizing a Refutation or Confirmation

Below is the organization pattern for a composition of this type.

1. Narrative	Here you narrate the events that you are going to discuss. • For example, in a court of law, the lawyer would lay out for the jury the story of what happened.
2. Your Opinion	Here you indicate your opinion about what happened. • For example, in a court of law, the prosecutor would say the defendant was guilty, while the defense would say the defendant was not guilty.
3. Approaches 1st 2nd 3rd 4th	Use the four approaches to show that the narrative was: • Possible or Impossible • Probable or Improbable • Clear or Unclear • Consistent or Inconsistent These can be used in any order. Also, if one of them is not related to your topic, you do not have to use it.
4. Conclusion	Write a brief statement restating your opinion and recapping the approaches you used.

Model Confirmation

What Am I?

Narrative

In 1826, a book entitled *The Book of Riddles* contained the riddle below. Our job is to figure out what is being described. Here's the riddle:

In almost every house I'm seen,
    (No wonder then I'm common)
I'm neither man, nor maid, nor child,
    Nor yet a married woman.

I'm penniless and poor as Job,
    Yet such my pride by nature,
I always wear a kingly robe,
    Though a dependent creature.

Writer's Opinion

I believe the riddle is describing a cat.

Clear

In lines two and three, the speaker *clearly* states that he is not a human—neither man, maid (young woman), child, nor married woman. In addition, in the last line, he calls himself a "creature." This tells us that the speaker is not an object, but an animal of some kind.

Possible

Also, it is very *possible* the animal is a cat. For example, he states that he lives in houses and is referred to as "common." Indeed, the household cat is often called a "common cat." It is not, for instance, a special breed, such as a Siamese or Persian cat.

Probable

Next, some things suggest the speaker is *probably* a cat, as opposed to a dog. Dogs and cats can both be seen in houses, but of these two, the cat is the one with the reputation for being prideful. Most cat owners would tell you that cats are so prideful they almost act as if they own the house sometimes! Also, a cat can be so proud of its mousing abilities, that it will bring home its catch-for-the-day and lay it at its owner's feet!

Consistent

Last, the details of the riddle are *consistent* with the characteristics of a cat. For one thing, the speaker says he is "penniless" and "dependent." Though a cat is a proud animal, it does not, in fact, own anything. In addition, the largest member of the cat family, the lion, is often referred to as the "king of the jungle," and the speaker in the riddle states he wears a "kingly robe."

Conclusion

For these reasons, it is *possible, probable, clear,* and *consistent* that the riddle is describing a cat.

EXERCISE 7.2: Practice with Approaches to Refutation and Confirmation

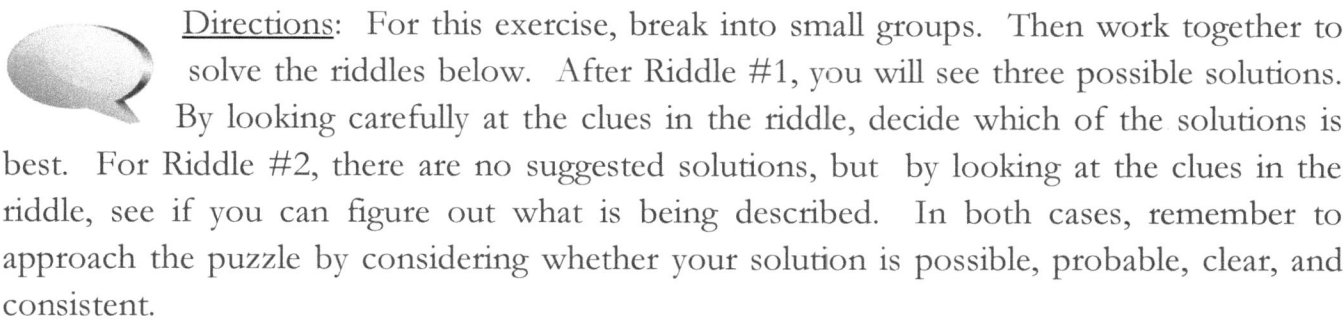

Directions: For this exercise, break into small groups. Then work together to solve the riddles below. After Riddle #1, you will see three possible solutions. By looking carefully at the clues in the riddle, decide which of the solutions is best. For Riddle #2, there are no suggested solutions, but by looking at the clues in the riddle, see if you can figure out what is being described. In both cases, remember to approach the puzzle by considering whether your solution is possible, probable, clear, and consistent.

Riddle #1
From the *Exeter Book* (10th-century England)

What Am I?

Christ, the commander   the true lord of victories,
ordained me for conflict.   I burn the living,
unnumbered people,   over all the earth.
I afflict them with pain,   though I never touch them,
whenever my Lord   bids me to battle.
Sometimes I gladden   the minds of many.
Sometimes I comfort   those I make war on,
even from afar.   They feel it nonetheless,
the hurt and the healing,   when now and again
over deep tribulation   I better their fortunes.[30]

Am I:

a. a king   b. a fire?   c. the sun?

Riddle #2
What Am I?

Through all my days, I've sore been pressed,
    And trampled under feet;
Stranger alike to joy and rest,
    Or liberty so sweet.

At length, I'm gone and quite decay'd,
    And nought can me condole;
For he whose power and wisdom made
    Me—cannot save my sole!

Answer: *a shoe*

Quills #1

Choose your solution to either Riddle #1 or Riddle #2 and write a confirmation, proving your solution is correct. Use the four approaches: Possible, Probable, Clear, and Consistent. Follow the pattern of the model composition explaining the cat riddle.

Model Refutation

Refutation of Geoffrey of Monmouth

Narrative

In the twelfth century, Geoffrey of Monmouth wrote a book entitled *History of the Kings of Britain*. In that book, Geoffrey claimed that Britain was founded by descendants of the ancient Trojans, specifically by Brutus (or Brute the Trojan), a descendant of Aeneas. According to Geoffrey, before Brute was born, a wizard foretold that he would have troubles but would eventually receive great honors. Accordingly, Brut was exiled from Italy but was told by the goddess Diana that the island of Albion (now Britain) was to be his. After arriving on the promised island, Brute and his men chased away the giants who lived there and settled down to live in Britain, which Geoffrey said was named after Brute himself.

Teacher's Edition

Writer's Position

Geoffrey's tale is just that—a tale, a legend. It is not actual history.

Improbable

<u>First</u>, the story is improbable. Brute was probably not even a real person. Geoffrey said that Brute was a descendant of Aeneas, but Aeneas was a fictional character who appeared in two epic poems. The first was Homer's famous legend, the *Iliad*, which was written in Greece about 1250 BC. The second was Virgil's *Aeneid*, which was written in Italy in about 20 BC. Since Aeneas was not a real person, Brute was probably not real either.

Unclear

<u>Second</u>, some elements of the story are very unclear. For example, Geoffrey states that Brute spent time on the island of Leogecia in the Mediterranean. Now, the Mediterranean region was well-mapped in ancient times. If Leogecia were a real place, its location would have been mapped long ago, yet it appears on no map and is not mentioned in any work other than Geoffrey's. Therefore, Brute's route to Britain from Italy is very unclear.

Inconsistent

<u>In addition</u>, some things in the tale are not consistent. For example, when the goddess Diana supposedly spoke to Brute in a dream, she indicated that the island "was once inhabited by giants." This suggests that the giants were no longer there, but when Brute arrived, his first challenge, according to Geoffrey, was to chase the giants into mountain caves. Thus, the information about the giants is inconsistent.

Impossible

<u>Last</u>, some parts of Geoffrey's tale are just impossible. For example, there is no such thing as wizards who can predict a person's future. The presence of such an element in the tale makes it impossible to believe.

Conclusion

<u>In short</u>, since Geoffrey's tale has elements that are <u>improbable</u>, <u>unclear</u>, <u>inconsistent</u>, and <u>impossible</u>, we must conclude that it is just a story, not a true history of Britain.

WHAT TO NOTICE:

1. **Introduction:** Identify each element of the narrative.

    a. *Who* is the narrative about (in other words, who is the hero of this narrative)?

    Brute, a descendant of the Trojan Aeneas

    b. *What* did Geoffrey of Monmouth say this hero did?

    He founded the country of Britain

    c. A specific date is not given to tell *when* this happened, but which of the following seems to best capture Geoffrey's meaning?

    __X__ It happened many centuries before Christ (BC).

    _____ It happened during the lifetime of the poet Virgil.

    d. *Where* did Brute supposedly land?

    On the island of Albion, which he re-named Britain

    e. *Why* did Brute go to that particular island?

    The goddess Diana promised it to him in a dream.

    f. *How* did Brute arrive?

    By ship, traveling through the Mediterranean from Italy.

2. **Writer's Opinion:** Does the writer of the model essay agree or disagree with Geoffrey of Monmouth's claim?

    The writer of the model essay disagrees.

3. **Improbable:** Why does the writer of the model essay say it is improbable that a Trojan founded Britain?

    It's improbable because Aeneas, his supposed ancestor, was a fictional character.

Teacher's Edition

4. **Unclear:** According to the writer of the model essay, what is not clear?

   The location of Leogecia, which Brute supposedly visited, is unclear.

5. **Inconsistent:** What inconsistency does the writer point out?

   Geoffrey made inconsistent remarks about giants. First he said they had "once" inhabited Britain, but when Brute arrived, the giants were still living there.

6. **Impossible:** What part of Geoffrey's narrative is impossible, according to the writer of the model essay?

   Wizards do not actually exist, so that part of the story is impossible.

7. **Conclusion:** In the conclusion, underline the four words that recap the four approaches used in the essay.

8. **Organization:** Underline the transition that begins each of the approaches and the conclusion.

Applying Refutation and Confirmation to Literature

We are fortunate in our country to have a system of law in which a defendant is considered innocent until proven guilty. This is a tradition that originated in England. Being punished for a crime one did not commit is probably one of the greatest injustices that can happen. Almost no one is willing to take another person's punishment. Therefore, it is not surprising that stories of wrongful accusations appear in the literature of England and the United States, countries that cherish the innocent-until-proven-guilty principle.

EXERCISE 7.3: Practice Refuting a Narrative

<u>Directions</u>: Please read the introductory note. Then read the excerpt from *Oliver Twist* by Charles Dickens and answer the questions that follow.

NOTE: The British author Charles Dickens (1812-1870), famous for his novel A Christmas Carol, *once wrote a novel called* The Adventures of Oliver Twist. *This novel is about a good kid who is thrown out of an orphanage for daring to ask for more food! He ends up homeless in London and is taken in by a disreputable character named Fagin, who gives homeless boys food and a place to sleep if they will go out onto the streets and pick pockets for him. The first time Oliver goes out with two other boys, Charley Bates and a character called the Artful Dodger, he is wrongfully accused of pickpocketing. We pick up the story where the three are standing across the street from an outdoor bookstall.*

Charles Dickens
1812-1870

Excerpt from *Oliver Twist*
By Charles Dickens

[1]

"What's the matter?" demanded Oliver.

"Hush!" replied the Dodger. "Do you see that old cove at the book-stall?"

"The old gentleman over the way?" said Oliver. "Yes, I see him."

"He'll do," said the Dodger.

"A prime plant," observed Master Charley Bates.

Oliver looked from one to the other, with the greatest surprise; but he was not permitted to make any inquiries; for the two boys walked stealthily across the road, and slunk close behind the old gentleman towards whom his attention had been directed. Oliver walked a few paces after them; and, not knowing whether to advance or retire, stood looking on in silent amazement.

The old gentleman was a very respectable-looking personage, with a powdered head and gold spectacles. He was dressed in a bottle-green coat with a black velvet collar; wore white trousers; and carried a smart bamboo cane under his arm. He had taken up a book from the stall, and there he stood, reading away, as hard as if he were in his elbow-chair, in his own study. . . .

What was Oliver's horror and alarm as he stood a few paces off, looking on with his eyelids as wide open as they would possibly go, to see the Dodger plunge his hand into the old gentleman's pocket, and draw from thence a handkerchief! To see him hand the same to Charley Bates; and finally to behold them, both, running away round the corner at full speed.

In an instant the whole mystery of the handkerchiefs, and the watches, and the Jewels, and the Jew [Fagin], rushed upon the boy's mind. He stood, for a moment, with the blood so tingling through all his veins from terror, that he felt as if he were in a burning fire; then, confused and frightened, he took to his heels; and, not knowing what he did, made off as fast as he could lay his feet to the ground.

This was all done in a minute's space. In the very instant when Oliver began to run, the old gentleman, putting his hand to his pocket, and missing his handkerchief, turned sharp round. Seeing the boy scudding away at such a rapid pace, he very naturally concluded him to be the depredator; and, shouting "Stop thief" with all his might, made off after him, book in hand.

[Oliver is apprehended by the police, identified by the old gentleman, and taken to a nearby police court, where he is put in a holding cell. We proceed to an excerpt from Chapter 11.]

[2]

This cell was in shape and size something like an area cellar, only not so light. It was most intolerably dirty; for it was Monday morning; and it had been tenanted by six drunken people, who had been locked up, elsewhere, since Saturday night. But this is little. In our station-houses, men and women are every night confined on the most trivial charges—the word is worth noting—in dungeons, compared with which, those in Newgate, occupied by the most atrocious felons, tried, found guilty, and under sentence of death, are palaces. Let any one who doubts this, compare the two.

The old gentleman looked almost as rueful as Oliver when the key grated in the lock. He turned with a sigh to the book, which had been the innocent cause of all this disturbance.

"There is something in that boy's face," said the old gentleman to himself as he walked slowly away, tapping his chin with the cover of the book, in a thoughtful manner; "something that touches and interests me. Can he be innocent? He looked like—By the bye," exclaimed the old gentleman, halting very abruptly, and staring up into the sky, "Bless my soul! Where have I seen something like that look before?"

[Time passes and Oliver is taken before a judge.]

[3]

The office was a front parlour, with a panelled wall. Mr. Fang sat behind a bar, at the upper end; and on one side the door was a sort of wooden pen in which poor little Oliver was already deposited: trembling very much at the awfulness of the scene.

Mr. Fang was a lean, long-backed, stiff-necked, middle-sized man, with no great quantity of hair, and what he had, growing on the back and sides of his head. His face was stern, and much flushed. If he were really not in the habit of drinking rather more than was exactly good for him, he might have brought an action against his countenance for libel, and have recovered heavy damages.

The old gentleman bowed respectfully; and advancing to the magistrate's desk, said, suiting the action to the word, "That is my name and address, sir." He then withdrew a pace or two; and, with another polite and gentlemanly inclination of the head, waited to be questioned. . . .

"Who are you?" said Mr. Fang.

The old gentleman pointed, with some surprise, to his card.

"Officer!" said Mr. Fang, tossing the card contemptuously away with the newspaper. "Who is this fellow?"

"My name, sir," said the old gentleman, speaking like a gentleman, "my name, sir, is Brownlow. Permit me to inquire the name of the magistrate who offers a gratuitous and unprovoked insult to a respectable person, under the protection of the bench." Saying this, Mr. Brownlow looked round the office as if in search of some person who would afford him the required information.

"Officer!" said Mr. Fang, throwing the paper on one side, "What's this fellow charged with?"

"He's not charged at all, your worship," replied the officer. "He appears against the boy, your worship."

His worship knew this perfectly well; but it was a good annoyance, and a safe one.

"Appears against the boy, does he?" said Fang, surveying Mr. Brownlow contemptuously from head to foot. "Swear him!"

"Before I am sworn, I must beg to say one word," said Mr. Brownlow: "and that is, that I really never, without actual experience, could have believed—"

"Hold your tongue, sir!" said Mr. Fang, peremptorily.

"I will not, sir!" replied the old gentleman.

"Hold your tongue this instant, or I'll have you turned out of the office!" said Mr. Fang. "You're an insolent, impertinent fellow. How dare you bully a magistrate!"

"What!" exclaimed the old gentleman, reddening.

"Swear this person!" said Fang to the clerk. "I'll not hear another word. Swear him."

Mr. Brownlow's indignation was greatly roused; but reflecting perhaps, that he might only injure the boy by giving vent to it, he suppressed his feelings and submitted to be sworn at once.

"Now," said Fang. "What's the charge against this boy? What have you got to say, sir?"

"I was standing at a book-stall—" Mr. Brownlow began.

"Hold your tongue, sir," said Mr. Fang. "Policeman! Where's the policeman? Here, swear this policeman. Now, policeman, what is this?"

The policeman, with becoming humility, related how he had taken the charge; how he had searched Oliver, and found nothing on his person; and how that was all he knew about it.

"Are there any witnesses?" inquired Mr. Fang.

"None, your worship," replied the policeman.

Mr. Fang sat silent for some minutes, and then, turning round to the prosecutor, said in a towering passion,

"Do you mean to state what your complaint against this boy is, man, or do you not? You have been sworn. Now, if you stand there, refusing to give evidence, I'll punish you for disrespect to the bench; I will, by—"

By what, or by whom, nobody knows, for the clerk and jailor [*sic*] coughed very loud, just at the right moment; and the former dropped a heavy book upon the floor, thus preventing the word from being heard—accidentally, of course.

With many interruptions, and repeated insults, Mr. Brownlow contrived to state his case; observing that, in the surprise of the moment, he had run after the boy because he saw him running away; and expressing his hope that, if the magistrate should believe him, although not actually the thief, to be connected with thieves, he would deal as leniently with him as justice would allow.

"He has been hurt already," said the old gentleman in conclusion. "And I fear," he added, with great energy, looking towards the bar, "I really fear that he is ill."

[Much time is wasted trying to determine if Oliver really needs a glass of water or if he is only pretending to be faint. Then, the "trial" continues.]

[4]

"How do you propose to deal with the case, sir?" inquired the clerk in a low voice.

"Summarily," replied Mr. Fang. "He stands committed for three months—hard labour of course. Clear the office."

The door was opened for this purpose, and a couple of men were preparing to carry the insensible boy to his cell; when an elderly man of decent but poor appearance, clad in an old suit of black, rushed hastily into the office, and advanced towards the bench.

"Stop, stop! Don't take him away! For Heaven's sake stop a moment!" cried the newcomer, breathless with haste.

Although the presiding Genii in such an office as this, exercise a summary and arbitrary power over the liberties, the good name, the character, almost the lives, of Her Majesty's subjects, especially of the poorer class; and although, within such walls, enough fantastic tricks are daily played to make the angels blind with weeping; they are closed to the public, save through the medium of the daily press. Mr. Fang was consequently not a little indignant to see an unbidden guest enter in such irreverent disorder.

"What is this? Who is this? Turn this man out. Clear the office!" cried Mr. Fang.

"I_will_speak," cried the man; "I will not be turned out. I saw it all. I keep the bookstall. I demand to be sworn. I will not be put down. Mr. Fang, you must hear me. You must not refuse, sir."

The man was right. His manner was determined; and the matter was growing rather too serious to be hushed up.

"Swear the man," growled Mr. Fang, with a very ill grace. "Now, man, what have you got to say?"

"This," said the man: "I saw three boys: two others and the prisoner here: loitering on the opposite side of the way, when this gentleman was reading. The robbery was committed by another boy. I saw it done; and I saw that this boy was perfectly amazed and stupefied by it." Having by this time recovered a little breath, the worthy book-stall keeper proceeded to relate, in a more coherent manner, the exact circumstances of the robbery.

"Why didn't you come here before?" said Fang, after a pause.

"I hadn't a soul to mind the shop," replied the man. "Everybody who could have helped me, had joined in the pursuit. I could get nobody till five minutes ago; and I've run here all the way."

"The prosecutor was reading, was he?" inquired Fang, after another pause.

"Yes," replied the man. "The very book he has in his hand."

"Oh, that book, eh?" said Fang. "Is it paid for?"

"No, it is not," replied the man, with a smile.

"Dear me, I forgot all about it!" exclaimed the absent old gentleman, innocently.

"A nice person to prefer a charge against a poor boy!" said Fang, with a comical effort to look humane. "I consider, sir, that you have obtained possession of that book, under very suspicious and disreputable circumstances; and you may think yourself very fortunate that the owner of the property declines to prosecute. Let this be a lesson to you, my man, or the law will overtake you yet. The boy is discharged. Clear the office."

Questions:

1. In Part 1, why did Mr. Brownlow think it was *possible* that Oliver had stolen his handkerchief?

   He saw him running away after the incident.

2. Why can the reader be sure that it was *impossible* for Oliver to have stolen the handkerchief? *The reader knows with certainty that Oliver watched the whole thing from across the street and was horrified because the narrator made it clear.*

3. In Part 2, Mr. Brownlow seems to question whether it is *probable* that Oliver stole the handkerchief. Why is that?

   Oliver has an innocent look about him and reminds Mr. Brownlow of someone he knows.

Teacher's Edition

4. In Part 3, does the policeman's testimony make it seem *clear* or *unclear* that Oliver stole the handkerchief? Why is that?

   It makes it unclear because no handkerchief was found on Oliver.

5. At the beginning of Part 4, Mr. Fang sentences Oliver to three months of hard labor. In your opinion, was his decision based on what was possible, probable, clear, and consistent? Why or why not? *The only thing that makes the charge look possible is that Mr. Brownlow saw him running. However, it certainly was not clear that he stole anything because the handkerchief was not on him, and his innocent appearance is not consistent with that of a hardened boy of the streets. Answers will vary as to whether or not the charge against Oliver was probable.*

6. What important information is added at the last minute by the bookseller? How and why does this change things? *The bookseller testifies that he saw other boys commit the crime. This changes things because now it is clear that someone else committed the crime. Oliver is released. The bookseller's testimony is consistent with the fact that the handkerchief was not in Oliver's possession.*

Quills #2

Pretend that you are an attorney who is going to speak in defense of Oliver Twist. You have done your homework: (a) you have talked to the bookseller, (b) you have talked to the police, (c) and you have heard out Mr. Brownlow, who seems to have a sense of Oliver's good character. Write a speech to persuade the jury that Oliver Twist is innocent of the charge of theft. Use the approaches we have studied in this chapter: Impossible, Improbable, Unclear, and Inconsistent. Follow this organization pattern: Narrative, Opinion, Approaches, Conclusion.

COMMONPLACE

Chapter 8

Introduction

Above is a medieval illustration of Judas (on the right) counting his thirty pieces of silver, a scene from the Bible narrative about Judas' betrayal of Jesus (Luke 22:3-6). For this payment, Judas willingly led the authorities to the Garden of Gethsemane and, by kissing Jesus, identified him to those who had come to arrest him.

Now, Judas had been one of Jesus' apostles from early in Jesus' ministry. He was even trusted as the treasurer of the disciples' money, and the others would probably have considered him a true friend. But, in his heart, he had a grudge—planted there by Satan, we are told—and at the Last Supper he saw his chance to make some money by betraying Jesus. For this terrible act of betrayal, the name of Judas has become a synonym for *traitor* throughout the world.

People everywhere—Christian and non-Christian alike—would probably agree that betrayal of a friend is a blameworthy action. Judas himself regretted what he did so much that he returned the money to the authorities and then went out and killed himself.

To write about such inexcusable human behaviors, the ancients created an exercise called the Commonplace. The purpose of this chapter is to introduce you to the Commonplace and give you a chance to practice it.

THINK IT THROUGH:

- As a class, think of other stories about betrayal you have read about or seen in movies.

- You do not have to give an oral answer to this question, but just think about it: Has anyone ever betrayed your trust? If so, how did it make you feel?

Definition and Purpose

- A *Commonplace* is a speech or composition in which one condemns an awful act and calls for some kind of punishment.

- Unlike the Invective, the Commonplace does not criticize a particular person who committed the sin, but the sin itself. Sometimes a stereotype will be presented, and the audience will be encouraged not to "be that guy."

Teacher's Edition

- The purpose of a Commonplace is to oppose an illegal act (such as theft) or a legal, but unworthy act (such as name-calling).

- Why is this exercise called a Commonplace? It is called Commonplace because it opposes acts which are *commonly* understood to be wrong. As writers, we do not have to persuade the readers that an act like theft is wrong. They just know it. The writer's job is to call for punishment.

Commonplace in Different Epochs

In popular culture today, we often hear someone describe a person whose behavior is not desirable. We might hear people complain about the "couch potato," the "loudmouth," or the "mooch." After the person's behavior is described, it is often followed by the admonition, "Don't be *that* guy!" Though this popular phrase may be the latest incarnation of the Commonplace, it definitely has its roots in ancient times. Both the Old and the New Testaments employ the elements of Commonplace, warning folks "not to be that guy" in terms of the life lived for God. The exercise below gives you a chance to examine some of those.

EXERCISE 8.1: Commonplace in the Bible

Directions: Below are some Bible passages which employ Commonplace. Please look up each one and in the blanks indicate the teaching of the Commonplace in your own words. The first one serves as an example.

1. **Passage:** Matthew 6:5

   "And when you pray, you must not be like the hypocrites. For they love to stand and pray in the synagogues and at the street corners, that they may be seen by others. Truly, I say to you, they have received their reward."

Commonplace:

Don't be like the *hypocrites* who *pray in public places hoping to impress others with their righteousness.*

2. **Passage:** I Peter 4:3-5

   Commonplace:

   Don't be like the *pagans* who *live a wild life.*

3. **Passage:** Matthew 23: 2-7

   Commonplace:

   Don't be like the *scribes and Pharisees* who *don't practice what they preach.*

Teacher's Edition

4. **Passage:** Proverbs 1:10-16

   Commonplace:

   Don't be like the _sinners_ who _practice violence and robbery._

Approaches to the Commonplace

Below is a chart that explains the five approaches to the Commonplace:

Contrast	Make a statement about the opposite of the virtue or vice.
	**Example:** If you are writing about the vice of lying, you would state that the opposite of lying is telling the truth.

Comparison	Compare the vice to something that is similar but even worse.
	**Example:** Lying is similar to fraud.

Commonplace | 121

Cause	Explain why someone might actually commit the sin.
	Example: People sometimes lie to avoid punishment, to win some advantage for themselves—or just to get attention.

Example	Offer an example of the vice you are describing. The Bible, history books, literature, and newspapers are good sources of examples.
	Example: One example of a character who lied to make himself seem important was the little boy who cried, "Wolf!"

Call for Punishment	Explain why the vice should be punished. One persuasive method is to describe the effect the vice had on other people.
	Example: A liar who gave false testimony at a trial might have caused the false imprisonment of an innocent person.

Organization

Although it is possible to use each of the approaches, some writers choose those approaches which are the strongest. These approaches will become the body of your essay. The best organization plan is as follows:

Teacher's Edition

1. Provide a brief narrative.

    - If the Commonplace is inspired by a particular incident, briefly explain what happened.

    - If more general in nature, make a statement about the virtue or vice you will discuss. A quotation or proverb on the subject is a helpful technique.

    - Commonplace permits the use of a general reference to the class of wrongdoer ("sinners," "hypocrites," etc.) as shown in the Bible excerpts in Exercise 8.1.

3. State your opinion clearly.
4. Write one well-developed paragraph for each approach you use.
5. Write a conclusion in which you recap the approaches you used.

Model Commonplace

Against Ingratitude

Narrative + Writer's Opinion

Well-known Christian evangelist Billy Graham once called ingratitude "one of the most vicious sins."[31] The great writer William Shakespeare also recognized the poison of ingratitude, especially in his play *King Lear*, where the king utters his famous line:

> How sharper than a serpent's tooth it is
> To have a thankless child.[32]

From the time that children are first able to understand speech, their parents teach them the "magic words" *please* and *thank you*, yet sadly many grow up and do not put the teaching into practice. <u>Ingratitude is a fault that all of us should avoid.</u>

Comparison

Ingratitude is similar to scorn. The *Merriam-Webster Dictionary* defines *scorn* as "a feeling that someone or something is not worthy of any respect or approval."[33] In Psalm 22, the psalmist anticipated the words of Jesus on the cross: "I am a worm and not a man, scorned by mankind and despised by the people" (v. 6). During his ministry, Jesus healed the sick, gave sight to the blind, and raised the dead, yet people were ungrateful. They scorned him, spat on him, beat him, and crucified him. Their scorn was a horrible form of ingratitude.

Contrast

The opposite of ingratitude is gratitude, showing thankfulness. The person who shows gratitude will write thank you notes for gifts and acts of kindness, will find a way to return a favor, and will learn to put others before self. While ingratitude creates hurt feelings, gratitude creates happiness.

Example

One of the most famous examples of ingratitude is revealed in Luke 17:11-19. In this passage, Luke tells about the time when lepers met Jesus as he entered a village. They rushed up to him, begging to be healed. He told them to go show themselves to the priests. Luke records, "And as they went, they were cleansed." Thus, when they reached the priests, the horrible disease had been lifted from them. Nine ran off jubilant, and only one returned to thank Jesus for healing him. Only one showed gratitude.

Cause

The cause of ingratitude is selfishness. Ungrateful people focus only on the pleasure they receive from someone's kindness. They enjoy grandma's Thanksgiving dinner, the ride home in a rainstorm, the allowance mom and dad give every Saturday morning, but they never stop to think how many hours grandma spent in the kitchen, how far out of the way the driver went, or how hard the parents have worked to be able to provide the money. Taking without saying thanks is caused by selfishness.

Call for Punishment

Though ingratitude is a vice rather than a crime, there still needs to be a consequence. After all, it is actually an act of love to hold people accountable if their acts hurt the feelings of another person. How might ungratefulness impact a kind person? What about the fellow who helps out his cousin but finds his cousin unwilling to help him out in return?

Or what about the girl who shares her lunch with a friend whose mom didn't send a lunch? If the friend snarfs up the lunch and then runs off to leave the helpful girl to play alone on the playground, how would the helpful girl feel? Would these people perhaps be less likely to help out in the future? And, if so, would that lead to a general decay in the friendliness of the town? Parents, schools, and churches are right to ask ungrateful people to apologize and perhaps to do an act of service for someone in need. Such measures might inspire the ungrateful person to be more thankful in the future.

Conclusion

In conclusion, ingratitude is one of the worst sins. It has been acknowledged to be so in the Bible and in the world's great literature. People who allow selfishness to drive their response to kindness need to be confronted in the hope that they can change.

EXERCISE 8.2: Analyzing a Commonplace

Directions: Analyze "Against Ingratitude" by answering the following questions.

1. Look first at the Narrative + Writer's Opinion.

    a. The writer begins by offering famous quotations. What two persons are quoted?

    Billy Graham and William Shakespeare

    b. Underline the sentence which contains the writer's own position.

2. In Comparison, the writer compares ingratitude to *betrayal*.

3. In Contrast, the writer contrasts ingratitude with showing *thankfulness*.

4. What Bible narrative is recounted in the Example?

    The narrative of the ten lepers healed by Jesus

5. a. In the Call for Punishment, what milder synonym for *punishment* is used in the first sentence?

b. In your own words, summarize the author's idea about how a helpful person might be impacted by ingratitude.

Answers will vary, but the basic idea is that a person might be less likely to offer help in the future.

EXERCISE 8.3: Brainstorming Contrast and Comparison

Directions: With a partner, brainstorm some ideas for Commonplace compositions. At the left, you will see a vice. In the other two columns, suggest behaviors that would serve as contrasts and comparisons. The first one serves as an example. *NOTE TO TEACHERS: Answers will vary. Some suggestions are listed below.*

Vice	Contrast (Opposite Behavior)	Comparison (Similar but Worse Behavior)
Disobedience to Parents	Obedience to parents	Disobedience to the law
Littering	Being tidy, cleaning up after oneself	Polluting water and air
Snubbing someone at the lunch table or in the halls	Being friendly, including everyone	Ignoring someone in need
Pushing a smaller child around on the playground	Assisting those who are weaker	Strong arm robbery

Teacher's Edition

EXERCISE 8.4: Brainstorming Examples

With a partner or with the class-at-large, brainstorm examples for the following vices. Your example can be from real life or from a book you have read. The first one serves as an example.

Vice	Example
Betrayal	*Judas' betrayal of Jesus for 30 pieces of silver*
Destroying property of others	*Answers will vary.*
Lying	*Answers will vary.*
Taking advantage of other people's kindness	*Answers will vary.*

Quills #1

Your teacher will give you the instructions you need to write a Commonplace.

COMPARISON

Chapter 9

Introduction

Most of us know the story from Grimm's fairy tales called "Little Red Riding Hood," which tells the tale of a girl who encounters a wolf in the woods while taking some food to her grandmother's house. The wolf beats her to the house, gobbles up the grandmother, and pretends to be the grandmother when Little Red arrives. The heart of the story goes like this:

> Little Red Riding Hood was surprised to find the cottage-door standing open, and when she went into the room, she had such a strange feeling that she said to herself, oh dear, how uneasy I feel to-day, and at other times I like being with grandmother so much.
>
> She called out, "Good morning," but received no answer. So she went to the bed and drew back the curtains. There lay her grandmother with her cap pulled far over her face, and looking very strange.
>
> "Oh, grandmother," she said, "what big ears you have."
>
> "The better to hear you with, my child," was the reply.

"But, grandmother, what big eyes you have," she said.

"The better to see you with, my dear."

"But, grandmother, what large hands you have."

"The better to hug you with."

"Oh, but, grandmother, what a terrible big mouth you have."

"The better to eat you with."

And scarcely had the wolf said this, than with one bound he was out of bed and swallowed up Little Red Riding Hood.[34]

Fortunately, a woodsman happens upon the scene and is able to rescue Little Red and her grandmother by the skillful use of some scissors, and they all live happily ever after—except the wolf, of course, whose belly was filled with stones, according to the woodsman's sense of justice.

Now, at the base of this story is a writing technique called Comparison. When Little Red Riding Hood arrives at her grandmother's house, she begins to notice that things do not seem as they usually do, and she begins to list differences between what she usually saw and what she saw that day.

THINK IT THROUGH: With your classmates, make a list of all the comparisons that Little Red makes from the time she arrives at the cottage. (HINT: You should be able to find eight of them.) *(1) door open; (2) uneasy feeling; (3) no answer; (4) cap pulled down; (5) ears; (6) eyes; (7) hands; (8) mouth*

Definition and Purpose of Comparison

1. A Comparison is an essay or speech that lists and discusses similarities and/or differences between two subjects.

2. The progymnasmata teachers suggested subjects such as the following:

   - Two people
   - Two things

- Two occasions (such as holidays)

- Two activities (such as sports)

- Two animals (species or individual animals)

- Two plants

3. The Greek teacher Aphthonius showed that Comparison is related to Encomium and Invective because we often praise or blame the things we compare.

 **THINK IT THROUGH:**

- If we compared the wolf and the grandmother from the story of "Little Red Riding Hood," which character would come in for praise and which for blame?

- What character traits of each might we logically assume to be different?

4. In our own times, textbook writers often compare two things in order to instruct their readers. For example, the science textbook might compare different kinds of clouds. In this case, praise or blame is not normally used.

 **THINK IT THROUGH:**

- In science class, what two animals could you compare?

- In geography, what two mountain ranges could you compare?

- In music class, what two musical instruments could you compare?

EXERCISE 9.1: Analyzing a Biblical Comparison

 Directions: In the New Testament book of Matthew, we find a narrative in which Jesus used Comparison to make a point. Please begin by reading the passage and then answer the questions that follow.

Build Your House on the Rock
Matthew 7:24-27

²⁴ "Everyone then who hears these words of mine and does them will be like a wise man who built his house on the rock. ²⁵ And the rain fell, and the floods came, and the winds blew and beat on that house, but it did not fall, because it had been founded on the rock. ²⁶ And everyone who hears these words of mine and does not do them will be like a foolish man who built his house on the sand. ²⁷ And the rain fell, and the floods came, and the winds blew and beat against that house, and it fell, and great was the fall of it."

1. This passage is a double Comparison. Take a moment to examine both comparisons.

    a. First, Jesus compares two kinds of people who hear His words. What is the difference between them?

    One "does" what he hears, but one does not.

    b. Second, two types of builders are compared. What is the difference between them?

2. When the storm came, what happened to each house?

    a. The house on the rock ___*did not fall*___.

    b. The house on the sand ___*fell*___

3. Now, if the two builders represent two types of people who hear Jesus' words, what does the storm represent?

   Answers may vary, but basically the storm represents the troubles we face in life.

4. When the Bible teaches us to build our house on the Rock, who is the Rock?

   Jesus is the Rock.

5. Does this Comparison contain praise (Encomium) and blame (Invective)? Explain your answer. *Yes, the man who built the house on the rock is praised; the man who built the house on the sand is blamed. Also, the person who hears and does Jesus' word is praised; the person who hears but does not do Jesus' word is blamed.*

EXERCISE 9.2: Comparison Paragraph with "Zigzag" Organization

Directions: Please read the paragraph below about the authors Mark Twain and Robert Louis Stevenson and then answer the questions that follow.

Mark Twain and Robert Louis Stevenson

Mark Twain
1835-1910

Robert Louis Stevenson
1850-1894

(1) The American author Mark Twain and the Scottish author Robert Louis Stevenson are alike in several ways. (2) First, both are famous for writing what was called "adventures for boys." (3) For example, Twain wrote *The Adventures of Huckleberry Finn* and *The Adventures of Tom Sawyer*, which tell the adventures of two lads who live in Missouri along the Mississippi River. (4) Likewise, Stevenson wrote *Treasure Island* and *Kidnapped*, which are about British lads who have adventures on the high seas. (5) Second, Twain and Stevenson both wrote novels that were set in the Middle Ages. (6) For instance, Twain wrote *A Connecticut Yankee in King Arthur's Court*, which is a fanciful time travel story set in medieval England. (7) Similarly, Stevenson wrote *The Black Arrow*, which is set in fifteenth-century England during the Wars of the Roses. (8) Last, both authors did some non-fiction travel writing. (9) To be specific, Twain wrote *The Innocents Abroad*, which is about his travels with a group of Americans in Europe and the Holy Lands. (10) In much the same way, Stevenson wrote *Across the Plains*, which details his trip from New York to California by rail. (11) Fortunately, these two authors were once able to meet face-

to-face—but only for an hour on a park bench in New York.

Questions:

1. If your teacher desires, you can review zigzag organization by creating the zigzag scheme for "Mark Twain and Robert Louis Stevenson" on the chalkboard.

2. Sentence 1 is the topic sentence. If we consider "Mark Twain and Robert Louis Stevenson" to be the general topic, what is the controlling idea?

    . . . alike in several ways

3. What are the listing transitions that lead the reader from point to point?

    Sentence 2: *First*

    Sentence 5: *Second*

    Sentence 8: *Last*

4. What transitions are used to introduce the examples for each point?

    Sentence 3: *For example*

    Sentence 6: *For instance*

    Sentence 9: *To be specific*

5. What transitions are used to compare Stevenson to Twain?

    Sentence 4: *Likewise*

    Sentence 7: *Similarly*

    Sentence 10: *In much the same way*

6. What are the three similarities named in Sentences 2, 5, and 8?

    Sentence 2: *adventures for boys*

    Sentence 5: *stories set in the Middle Ages*

    Sentence 8: *non-fiction travel writing*

Teacher's Edition

Approaches to Comparison

1. For starters, we can refer to the advice of the Greek teacher Aphthonius, who pointed out that a writer can compare the following:

   - Two praiseworthy people or things

   - Two blameworthy people or things

   - A praiseworthy person or thing to a blameworthy person or thing

    **THINK IT THROUGH:** With your classmates, brainstorm pairs of praiseworthy people or fictional characters from history or literature who would make good subjects for comparison.

2. Aphthonius also said that if we write about persons, we can use the approaches we used in Encomium and Invective:

   - Similar characteristics (virtues or vices)

   - Similar deeds (good or evil)

   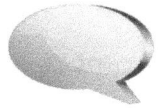 **THINK IT THROUGH:** Can you think of two evil characters from fairy tales? In what ways were they similar?

3. Another classical teacher, Hermogenes, suggested comparing two activities, such as sports, games, clubs, music groups, and so on. In this case, he suggests the following topics:

   - Origins of the activities (place and date, if known)

   - Mental qualities (e.g., concentration or memory)

   - Physical qualities (e.g., speed in a sport, pitch in music)

 **THINK IT THROUGH:** Can you think of two sports or games that are similar? In what ways are they similar in mental qualities (brain work) and physical qualities (body work)?

EXERCISE 9.3: Practicing Transitions of Similarity

 Directions: Work with a partner to write sentences that make comparisons. You will need to write two sentences, one for each item. Remember to start the second sentence with the transition. The first one serves as an example.

1. Compare exercise and homework with respect to how they improve a person. (Use *similarly*).

 *Exercise improves the body. Similarly, homework improves the mind.*

2. Compare birds and fish with respect to how they move. (Use *in much the same way*.)

 *Birds move by using their wings. In much the same way, fish move by using their fins*

3. Compare a twelve-year-old boy to a seventeen-year-old boy with respect to transportation? (Use *likewise*.)

 *A twelve-year-old boy rides a bicycle. Likewise, a seventeen-year-old boy rides a motorcycle.*

4. Compare a wolf to a hippo with respect to the sounds they make. (Use *similarly.*)

  *A wolf howls. Similarly, a hippo roars.*

Model Comparison

Is the Loch Ness Monster a Plesiosaur?

Background + Narrative

The Loch Ness Monster has been classified as a cryptoid, an animal that has been seen but is unknown to science. Sightings of the monster have been recorded since AD 565, when St. Columba observed it in Loch Ness, which is a lake (*loch*) in the Scottish Highlands. There were two alleged land sightings in 1933, and then in 1934 a doctor named Robert Kenneth Wilson supposedly captured its image in a photograph (see at right). Arthur Grant, one of the persons who allegedly saw the creature on land in 1933, was a student of veterinary medicine, and he believed that the animal bore similarities to the prehistoric plesiosaurus (see below), a creature whose skeletal remains have been found in rock strata in the British Isles.

"THE SURGEON'S PHOTO" OF 1934

Comparisons ("Zigzag" Paragraph)

What exactly are the similarities between the cryptoid and the plesiosaurus? First, they are similar in size. The creature seen in or near Loch Ness has been estimated to

Plesiosaur on Land
by Heinrich Harder

be from 25 to 40 feet in length. <u>Similarly</u>, the largest plesiosaur discovered was 50 feet long, and the *elasmosaurus* (a sub-species) was about 45 feet long. Secondly, the body shape is similar. Arthur Grant said the creature had a bulky body, a long neck, a small head, and four huge paddle-like legs by which it moved. <u>Likewise</u>, the plesiosaurus had a rounded body, a 20-foot-long neck, and a very small head. A plesiosaur skeleton now in the University of Nebraska State Museum shows that the creatures also had four huge "paddles," which they may have used like wings to propel themselves through the water.[35] Third, both of these sea creatures seem to take in oxygen through lungs, not gills. For example, the supposed Loch Ness Monster is seen in the photo extending its long neck out of the air in order to breathe. <u>In much the same way</u>, the plesiosaurs are known to have breathed through lungs, not gills like fish.

Conclusion

Is there a creature living in Loch Ness? Is it a "grandchild" of the ancient plesiosaurus? These are questions which cannot be answered unless and until a specimen is captured and studied. Until then, it is just fun to speculate.

EXERCISE 9.4: Analyzing the Model Comparison

Directions: After reading the essay comparing the Loch Ness Monster to a plesiosaur, study it by answering the questions below.

1. The first sentence in Background + Narrative shows that one way to begin the Background is to provide:
   A. an example.
   B. <u>a definition.</u>
   C. a characteristic of the Loch Ness Monster.

2. The remainder of Background + Narrative tells:
   A. tales of terror about the monster.
   B. a description of the monster.
   C. <u>sightings of the monster.</u>

3. In Comparisons, what is the key word in the topic sentence (that is, the word that indicates the Controlling Idea)?
   A. <u>Similarities</u>
   B. Cryptoid
   C. Plesiosaur

4. In Comparisons, what are the three similarities that are discussed?

   "First, they are similar in <u>size</u>."

   "Secondly, the <u>body shape</u> is similar."

   "Third, both of these sea creatures seem to <u>take in oxygen through lungs, not gills</u>."

Teacher's Edition

5. Underline the three transitions that introduce the comparisons.

6. What did the writer conclude in the last paragraph of the essay?
    A. The Loch Ness Monster was indeed a plesiosaur.
    B. The Loch Ness Monster was not a plesiosaur.
    C. <u>We do not know if the monster is a plesiosaur.</u>

Quills #1

 Your teacher will give you the instructions you need to write a Comparison.

SPEECH-IN-CHARACTER

Chapter 10

Introduction

Below is a poem by A. E. Housman (1859-1936) from his famous collection called *A Shropshire Lad* (1896). Like this one, many of Housman's poems show how fleeting happiness can be. At the time Housman was writing, World War I was still in the future, but when it did come, the British realized that a number of the poems from *A Shropshire Lad* expressed the feelings of many soldiers going off to war.

XL

Into my heart an air that kills
  From yon far country blows:
What are those blue remembered hills,
  What spires, what farms are those?

That is the land of lost content,
  I see it shining plain,
The happy highways where I went
  And cannot come again.[36]

A. E. Housman
1859-1936

THINK IT THROUGH:

- What seems to be happening in this poem?
- What mood does the speaker seem to be experiencing?

This short poem has the pattern of an element of the progymnasmata called Speech-in-Character. The purpose of this chapter is to introduce you to Speech-in-Character and give you an opportunity to practice writing one.

Definition and Purpose of Speech-in-Character

1. A Speech-in-Character is the speech of a character in a poem, play, story, or novel.

2. Its purpose is to reveal something about the personality of the speaker, especially when placed in a particularly joyous or difficult situation.

3. It is written in such a way that the word choice reflects the nature of the speaker. A soldier might not speak the same way as a dairy maid, for example.

Content of a Speech-in-Character

When you write a Speech-in-Character, you will begin by creating a character and putting him or her into some kind of situation. Some examples are the following:

- I'm in a bad situation. What got me into it? What can I do about it?
- I'm in a bad situation. What got me into it? What could make it even worse?
- I'm in a good situation. What has put me here? Can I maintain it?
- I'm in a good situation. What has put me here? What might make it even better?

As its name, *Speech-in-Character*, indicates, this type of composition depends on the creation of a character. It might be helpful to recall the topics for Character from Chapter 3:

Teacher's Edition

- Name

- Age

- Gender

- Nationality/Ethnic Group

- Appearance

- Mental/Emotional State

All of these are important when writing a Speech-in-Character because all these elements will influence how the character feels about and approaches his or her situation: past, present, and future. A young character might be filled with hope while an older one might realize that death is approaching, for example. One person might feel helpless in the same situation that would make another ready to fight. It will be important for you to put yourself into your character's shoes, so to speak, to understand and communicate what he or she feels.

EXERCISE 10.1: Thinking about Character

John Bunyan
1628-1688

Directions: Below are some paraphrased excerpts from *Pilgrim's Progress* (1678) by John Bunyan (1628-88). Please begin by reading the introductory note and the excerpts. The questions that follow will help you to see what Bunyan did to reveal each character's personality and attitude.

Excerpt #1

Note: The character named Christian, who represents all believers, is convinced from Scripture of his own sin and seeks to unburden himself. Evangelist tells him he needs to travel from the City of Destruction (the world) to the Celestial City (heaven), so he sets out on his journey. Along the way, he is beset by many characters such as Obstinate and Pliable, who try to persuade him to return. It is not long before he comes across the arch-devil Apollyon, whose name means "Destroyer." Apollyon asks Christian where he is going.

    CHRISTIAN: (1) I have come from the City of Destruction, which is the place of all evil, and am going to the City of Zion.

APOLLYON: (2) Then I see that you are one of my subjects, for all of that country is mine, and I am the prince and the god of it. (3) How come you have run away from your king? (4) If I didn't hope to get more work out of you, I'd strike you to the ground right now with one blow! . . . .

CHRISTIAN: (5) I was, indeed, born in your country, but your service was hard, and a man cannot live upon your wages, for the wages of sin is death. . . .

APOLLYON: (6) Well, since you complain of your service and wages, be content to go back, and I promise to give you what our country can afford.

CHRISTIAN: (7) But I have contracted with another—the King of princes, and how can I with fairness go back to you?

APOLLYON: (8) You contracted with Him, but it is like the old proverb, "You have gone from bad to worse." (9) Still, it isn't unusual for one of His servants to give Him the slip and return to me again. (10) Do so and all will be well. . . .

CHRISTIAN: (11) Give up trying to persuade me anymore. (12) I am His servant, and I will follow Him.

APOLLYON: (13) When you are not so worked up, think all of this over again—what you are likely to meet with in the way you are going. (14) You know that, for the most part, His servants come to a bad end because they go against me and my ways. (15) How many of them have been put to shameful deaths! (16) And, besides, you count His service better than mine, whereas He has never come from the place where He is to deliver anyone that served him out of the enemy's hands. (17) But, as for me, how many times—as all the world very well knows!—have I, either by power or trickery, freed my faithful servants from Him and His? (18) And, in the same way, I will deliver you.

1. What does Apollyon's statement in Sentence 4 tell you about his character?

    It shows Apollyon is a bully who will use violence.

2. John 8:44 tells us that Satan "is a liar and the father of lies." In Sentences 16–18, what lie does Apollyon tell? How do you know it is a lie?

    In Sentence 17, Apollyon says that God has never come from heaven to deliver anyone who served him. We know this is a lie because Jesus came to earth to die for our sins.

Teacher's Edition

3. What statement does Apollyon make in Sentence 17 that reveals his character?

He admits that he uses trickery to get things done.

Excerpt #2

Note: While traveling with Hope, Christian and Hope are taken prisoner by the Giant Despair, who beats them and locks them in a prison. Though the dungeon is "nasty and stinking," the Giant Despair has a weakness: When the sun is shining, he falls down in a fit and loses the use of his hands.

Christian and Hope in Prison

CHRISTIAN: (19) Brother, what shall we do? (20) The life that we now live is miserable. (21) For my part, I don't know if it is best to live this way or to die out of hand? (22) "I would choose strangling and death rather than my bones" (Job 7:15). (23) Should we let ourselves be ruled by the Giant?

HOPE: (24) Indeed, our present condition is dreadful, and death would be better than remaining in this dungeon, but don't forget what the Lord of the country we are going to has said: "You shall not murder." (25) We are not to kill another person, and much more we are forbidden to kill ourselves. (26) If a man kills another man, he kills the body, but if he kills himself, he kills both body and soul. (27) You talk about ease in the grave, but have you forgotten about hell where, for certain, murderers go? (28) "No murderer has eternal life abiding in him" (I John 3:15).

(29) Also, don't forget: not all the law is in the hand of Giant Despair. (30) He has taken others, not just us—and some have escaped from him. (31) Who knows? (32) It is possible that the God who made the world may cause the Giant Despair to die. (33) Or, the Giant could forget to lock us up one of these days. (34) Or, he may have another of his fits and lose the use of his arms and legs, like before. (35) So I am determined to pluck up the heart of a man and try my utmost to get out from under the Giant's hand. (36) I was foolish not to try it before, but let's be patient. (37) Let's wait a while. (38) The time may come when we may escape, but let's not become our own murderers.

1. At first, Sentences 24-28 do not sound hopeful. Why do you suppose the author wrote unhopeful things for Hope to say?

Answers may vary, but we know from Hope's quotation from Scripture that he is telling the truth. Hope cannot be separated from truth.

2. In Sentences 31-34, Hope offers several hopeful possibilities. What are they?

   a. Sentence 32: God may cause the Giant Despair to *die*.

   b. Sentence 33: The Giant could *forget to lock them up someday*.

   c. Sentence 34: The Giant could *have another fit and lose the use of his arms and legs*.

3. In Sentences 35-38, Hope says some things that reveal his character.

   a. Sentence 35: Hope says he is *determined to pluck up the heart of man*.

   b. Sentence 36: Hope shows that he has *patience*.

Verb Tense Options in a Speech-in-Character

The characters in *Pilgrim's Progress* use various time frames in their speeches. For example, Appolyon uses present tense to remind Christian that he *is* one of his subjects. Then he uses present perfect tense in his lie when he says that God *has never come* from heaven to help anyone.

Switching between time frames is not unusual for a Speech-in-Character. In fact, many speeches of this type occur when characters find themselves in some kind of predicament. They stop to think things over, and we listen as they state what their problem is (present tense), review how they got into the problem (past tense), and try to figure out how to get out of the problem (future tense).

Look at the poem below by Christina Rossetti (1830-94), in which the speaker of the poem uses this three-part approach when reflecting on her separation from God.

Teacher's Edition

Good Friday
By Christina Rossetti

Am I a stone, and not a sheep,
That I can stand, O Christ, beneath thy cross,
To number drop by drop Thy Blood's slow loss,
And yet not weep?
Not so those women loved

Who with exceeding grief lamented Thee;
Not so fallen Peter weeping bitterly;
Not so the thief was moved;

Not so the Sun and Moon
Which hid their faces in a starless sky,
A horror of great darkness at broad noon—
I, only I.

Yet give not o'er,
But seek Thy sheep, true Shepherd of the flock;
Greater than Moses, turn and look once more
And smite a rock.[37]

Christina Rossetti
1830-1894

THINK IT THROUGH:

- **Present tense:** (Stanza 1) How does the speaker characterize himself (or herself) while standing at the foot of the cross?

- **Past tense:** (Stanzas 2 and 3) Who differed from the speaker in the past? What features of Nature differed from the speaker?

- **Future tense:** (Stanza 4) What does the speaker ask God to do to bring about change?

Speech-in-Character | 147

Organizing a Speech-in-Character

Using the time-frame of Speech-in-Character, one can organize a Speech-in-Character by using this formula:

Present + Past + Future

1. **Present**: Here's my predicament.

2. **Past**: Here's how I got into my predicament.

3. **Future**: Here's what may happen next because of my predicament.

OR

Here's what I'm going to do to get out of my predicament.

EXERCISE 10.2: Examining a Speech-in-Character

Directions: Please begin by reading the introductory note. Then read the excerpt and answer the questions that follow.

Note: Henry Wadsworth Longfellow's epic poem, Evangeline (1847), *is set during a period in history called the Expulsion of the Acadians (1755-64). The Acadians were French-speaking colonists in areas today known as Nova Scotia, New Brunswick, and Prince Edward Island in Canada. The British had gained control of the area in 1713, but the Acadians had maintained their French identity and refused to swear loyalty to the English king. During the French and Indian War, which was the American extension of the war in Europe between England and France, the English expelled the Acadians. Longfellow's poem centers on the young Acadian woman Evangeline, whose sweetheart, Gabriel Lajeunesse, has been expelled into the interior of America. She spends years searching for him, sometimes missing him by just hours. The lines below contain Evangeline's Speech-in-Character from Part II of the poem, followed by the narrator's commentary.*

Statue of Evangeline
Martinville, Louisiana

Teacher's Edition

Excerpt from *Evangeline*
By Henry Wadsworth Longfellow

And the soul of the maiden, between the stars and the fire-flies,
Wandered alone, and she cried, "O Gabriel! O my beloved!
Art thou so near unto me, and yet I cannot behold thee?
Art thou so near unto me, and yet thy voice does not reach me?
Ah! how often thy feet have trod this path to the prairie! 5
Ah! how often thine eyes have looked on the woodlands around me!
Ah! how often beneath this oak, returning from labor,
Thou hast lain down to rest, and to dream of me in thy slumbers!
When shall these eyes behold, these arms be folded about thee?"
Loud and sudden and near the notes of a whippoorwill sounded 10
Like a flute in the woods; and anon, through the neighboring thickets,
Farther and farther away it floated and dropped into silence.
"Patience!" whispered the oaks from oracular caverns of darkness:
And, from the moonlit meadow, a sigh responded, "To-morrow!"[38]

Questions:

1. Line 2+:

    a. Starting with and including Line 2 (beginning with "O Gabrielle!"), which lines use present tense?

    Lines 2-4 use present tense.

    b. In your own words, summarize what Evangeline is thinking here.

    She thinks Gabriel might be near but she can't hear or see him.

2. Lines 5-8: These lines are in present perfect tense (e.g., *have trod*), which is sometimes used for the recent past. In your own words, write one sentence to indicate what Evangeline is thinking here as she reflects on the past few years.

    She wonders how often he has looked on the same things she is looking on, how often he has thought of her, etc.

3. Line 9:

a. What tense is used in Line 9? *Line 9 uses future tense.*

b. Again, in your own words, tell what Evangeline wonders here.

She wonders when she will see him again.

4. Lines 13-14:

   a. Who or what answers Evangeline's question from Line 9?

   Answers will vary, but basically Nature responds—first an oak, then a "sigh" (the wind?).

   b. What is the answer?

   She is told to be patient and to wait till "Tomorrow," which is probably a reference to the distant future, not a 24-hour cycle.

   c. Does the answer conform to the future time period, which is usually the third part of a Speech-in-Character?

   Yes.

5. Overall, how would you describe the mood or emotion that is revealed in Evangeline's words?

Answers will vary, but Evangeline shows some frustration about her seemingly hopeless situation.

EXERCISE 10.3: Examining a Speech-in-Character

 Directions: Please read the introductory note and the Speech-in-Character from a poem by William Blake. Then answer the questions which follow.

William Blake
1757-1827

Note: The English poet William Blake (1757-1827) lived in a time when many in Great Britain were speaking out against the slave trade. Though slavery was not legal in Great Britain, some persons captured in Africa and India had been brought back to England by their "masters." Eventually the British law needed to rule whether continuing to hold these slaves was legal (they decided it was not). Like many Christians of the period, William Blake opposed slavery out of his beliefs that all human beings had been created by God and that Jesus had died for all. In 1789, he published a poem which is in the form of a Speech-in-Character. The character is a Christian African child in England, who is enslaved.

The Little Black Boy
By William Blake

My mother bore me in the southern wild,
   And I am black, but O my soul is white!
White as an angel is the English child,
   But I am black, as if bereaved of light.

My mother taught me underneath a tree,   5
   And, sitting down before the heat of day,
She took me on her lap and kissed me,
   And, pointing to the East, began to say:

Look on the rising sun: there God does live,
   And gives His light, and gives His heat away,   10
And flowers and trees and beasts and men receive
   Comfort in morning, joy in the noonday.

And we are put on earth a little space,
   That we may learn to bear the beams of love;
And these black bodies and this sunburnt face   15
   Are but a cloud, and like a shady grove.

For, when our souls have learned the heat to bear,
   The cloud will vanish, we shall hear His voice,
Saying, "Come out from the grove, my love and care,
   And round my golden tent like lambs rejoice.   20

Thus did my mother say, and kissed me,
   And thus I say to little English boy.
When I from black, and he from white cloud free,
   And round the tent of God like lambs we joy,

> I'll shade him from the heat till he can bear 25
> To lean in joy upon our Father's knee;
> And then I'll stand and stroke his silver hair,
> And be like him, and he will then love me.[39]

Questions:

1. a. Which lines in the first stanza show the Present situation?

   Lines 2-4 show the Present situation.

   b. What is that situation?

   The speaker is a black child, but he has a "white" soul—perhaps meaning pure.

2. a. In Lines 5-21, what past event does the boy remember?

   He remembers a story his mother told him.

   b. What did the boy learn from his mother?

   He learned there was a God who would one day call them home.

3. In Lines 23-28, what does the speaker say he will now do with what he learned in the past?

   He will share the message with a white child.

4. a. What lines represent Future time?

   Lines 23-28 represent Future time.

   b. In Line 28, what does he say will happen?

   He says that when he and the white child are in heaven, he will shield the white child from the heat so that he (the white child) can enjoy God more. He says the white child will love him then.

5. What emotions does this poem create?

   Answers may vary, but one might see sadness, nostalgia, and hope in this poem.

Teacher's Edition

EXERCISE 10.4: Planning a Speech-in-Character

Directions: Below are some images from traditional works of fiction. With a partner, select two of them and brainstorm possible responses to the prompts that appear at the left.

Character:	1. 
Predicament:	
Cause of Predicament:	
Solution or Result of Predicament:	
Mood(s):	

Speech-in-Character | 153

Classical Quills II

Character:	2.
Predicament:	
Cause of Predicament:	
Solution or Result of Predicament:	
Mood(s):	

Character:	3.
Predicament:	
Cause of Predicament:	
Solution or Result of Predicament:	
Mood(s):	

Teacher's Edition

Character:	4.
Predicament:	
Cause of Predicament:	
Solution or Result of Predicament:	
Mood(s):	

Quills #1

 Your teacher will provide you with a composition assignment so that you can show your ability to write a Speech-in-Character.

Speech-in-Character | 155

THESIS

Chapter 11

Introduction

The Horse and the Stag
By Aesop

At one time the Horse had the plain entirely to himself. Then a Stag intruded into his domain and shared his pasture. The Horse, desiring to revenge himself on the stranger, asked a man if he were willing to help him in punishing the Stag. The man replied that if the Horse would receive a bit in his mouth and agree to carry him, he would contrive effective weapons against the Stag. The Horse consented and allowed the man to mount him. From that hour he found that instead of obtaining revenge on the Stag, he had enslaved himself to the service of man.[40]

The fable of "The Horse and the Stag" shows how one can be ruined by trying to take vengeance for an offense. It would plainly have been better for the Horse if he had just forgiven the Stag for entering his domain, but sometimes vengeance comes more easily than forgiveness.

We know what the Bible says about forgiving others, but most people still find it quite difficult to do. Imagine you were asked to present a Sunday School lesson about why people should practice forgiveness. In such a case, you would be presenting what the ancients called a Thesis. That is, you would be proposing a wise course of action and explaining why your listeners should accept your proposal.

To do this, you would benefit from knowing the various approaches to Thesis. The purpose of this chapter is to present those approaches and give you the chance to practice composing a Thesis.

Definition and Purpose

1. The Greek word *thesis* means a *proposition*, that is, an idea that someone *proposes*.

2. The Thesis, then, is a composition or speech in which the writer makes a proposal based on his or her opinion and knowledge of the subject.

3. The purpose of a Thesis is to persuade others to take a certain course of action.

Approaches to Thesis

This chapter introduces four approaches to Thesis. In this exercise, the word *approach* means about the same thing as a *reason*. In other words, there are four typical reasons a person can give for a proposal. One can ask:

Is the proposal . . .

- necessary or unnecessary?
- advantageous or disadvantageous?
- customary or not customary?
- just or unjust?

Teacher's Edition

Below is an explanation of each approach along with examples.

Necessary or Unnecessary	Explain why the action you propose is necessary, or explain why the action you oppose is unnecessary.
	**Example:** It is necessary for a Christian to practice forgiveness because Ephesians 4:32 commands us to do so: "Be kind to one another, tenderhearted, forgiving one another, as God in Christ forgave you."

Advantageous or Disadvantageous	Explain the advantages people would receive from the action you propose, or explain the disadvantages from the action you oppose.
	**Example:** Sincere forgiveness brings an advantage, as we learn in Matthew 6:14a: "For if you forgive others their trespasses, your heavenly Father will also forgive you."

Customary or Not Customary	Explain how the proposal does or does not fit with our customs (our usual way of doing things).
	**Example:** Forgiveness is customary among our institutions. For example, libraries sometimes forgive late fines, teachers sometimes cancel one bad test score, and judges sometimes exercise mercy.

Thesis | 159

Just or Unjust	Explain how the proposal is just (fair) or unjust (unfair).
	Example: According to 1 John 1:9a, there is justice in forgiveness, especially when the other person has apologized: "If we confess our sins, he is faithful and just to forgive us our sins."

IMPORTANT NOTE: Although the Greeks established several approaches to Thesis, it is not necessary to use all of them in any one composition. Rather, select those approaches which are best for the topic at hand.

EXERCISE 11.1: Identifying Approaches to Thesis

Theodore Roosevelt
1858-1919

Directions: Below are opinions expressed by President Theodore Roosevelt (1858-1919). Begin by reading the introductory note. Then read each excerpt. Following the excerpt, you will be asked which approach Roosevelt was using in the excerpt. Circle the correct answer.

Note: In May 1900, President Theodore Roosevelt published an article entitled "What We Can Expect of the American Boy" in St. Nicholas Magazine,[41] *a popular children's magazine of the day. A year before he published this article, he delivered a speech entitled "The Strenuous Life," in which he advocated "success which comes, not to the man who desires mere easy peace, but to the man who does not shrink from danger, from hardship, or from bitter toil. . . ." The St. Nicholas article is addressed to boys, reflecting the culture of the times. As you read, you may want to consider whether his thoughts apply not only to "good boys and good men," but also to "good girls and good women." You may wish to discuss this issue with your classmates.*

Teacher's Edition

Excerpts from "What We Can Expect of the American Boy"
By President Theodore Roosevelt

1. **Excerpt:** "Of course, what we have a right to expect of the American boy is that he shall turn out to be a good American man. Now, the chances are strong that he won't be much of a man *unless* he is a good deal of a boy. He *must not* be a coward or a weakling, a bully, a shirk, or a prig. He *must* work hard and play hard. He *must* be clean-minded and clean-lived, and able to hold his own under all circumstances and against all comers. It is *only on these conditions* that he will grow into the kind of American man of whom America can be really proud."

    Question: Review the italicized words, then choose the correct word to finish this sentence: Roosevelt believed that, for American boys to become good American men, certain things were (<u>necessary</u> / just).

2. **Excerpt:** "The great growth in the love of athletic sports, for instance, while fraught with danger if it becomes one-sided and unhealthy, has beyond all question had an excellent effect in increased manliness."

    Question: Here the President argues that sports are (customary for / <u>advantageous to</u>) boys.

3. **Excerpt:** "[T]o mis-estimate athletics is equally bad whether their importance is magnified or minimized. The Greeks were famous athletes, and as long as their athletic training had a normal place in their lives, it was a good thing. But it was a very bad thing when they kept up their athletic games while letting the stern qualities of soldiership and statesmanship sink into disuse."

    Question: In this statement, Roosevelt shows that over-emphasis on sports might be (<u>disadvantageous</u> / unjust).

4. **Excerpt:** "I am no advocate of senseless and excessive cramming in studies, but a boy should work, and should work hard, at his lessons—in the first place, for the sake of what he will learn, and in the next place, for the sake of the effect upon his own character of resolutely settling down to learn it. Shiftlessness, slackness, indifference in studying, are almost certain to mean inability to get on in other walks of life."

   Question: In this excerpt, Roosevelt says that studying hard is (<u>advantageous to</u> / customary for) the young.

5. **Excerpt:** "A healthy-minded boy should feel hearty contempt for the coward, and even more hearty indignation for the boy who bullies girls or small boys, or tortures animals."

   Question: Here Roosevelt argues that it is (customary / <u>just</u>) to stick up for victims of bullies.

Organizing a Thesis Essay

When writing an essay arguing for or against a proposition, follow this plan of organization:

1. **Introduction:** State the proposition in a neutral tone. That is, do not tip your hand right away as to whether you are for or against the idea.

2. **Narrative:** Provide narrative details so that the reader will be able to understand the question.

3. **Writer's Opinion:** State whether you are for or against the proposal.

4. **Arguments:** Choose those approaches which would best explain the reasons for your opinion and develop each in standard zigzag style. Each one will have its own paragraph.

5. **Conclusion:** Briefly drive home your point.

Teacher's Edition

Model Thesis Essay

Against Interactive Wildlife Sanctuaries

Introduction

Should animal sanctuaries and wildlife parks allow human interaction with species deemed harmless to humans?

Narrative

Animal sanctuaries are facilities where animals that have been abused or used in lab testing can go to live out their lives in a natural environment. These facilities are not open to the public and do not engage in animal breeding. There are also wildlife parks. In wildlife parks, some interaction between people and animals is allowed (for example, petting rabbits). These two groups often criticize each other's goals. The people who believe that humans should protect wildlife favor interaction. Those who think that the rights of an individual animal should never be violated prefer to keep animals away from humans.

Writer's Position

There are several reasons why animal sanctuaries should not allow human interaction.

Unjust

First and most importantly, interactive wildlife parks are unjust. If one particular animal must sit in a cage or live in a restricted area, it may help save the species, but the individual animal does not have the freedom it deserves. As Tim Harrison, who operates Outreach for Animals in Dayton, Ohio, said, "Sanctuaries should be a place for animals to retire. The animals should be respected, and not treated as a prop or an object."[42]

Necesary

Secondly, it has become necessary to have a safe place for rescued animals. Harvest Home Sanctuary in California, for example, tells the story of a little brown goat named Mocha. Since goats eat grass, a California family acquired Mocha to serve as its "living lawnmower." However, Mocha, being a goat, would climb up onto the rooftop, which the family considered a nuisance. They no longer wanted her. Harvest

Thesis | 163

 Home then took Mocha in, and she now roams the prairies "with her friend Selma the goat."[43] Without their help, Mocha would have been killed or placed in a cage for exhibition.

Conclusion

In conclusion, because zoos and wildlife parks do not consider the rights of an individual animal and because rescued animals need a safe place to live, interaction between animals and humans should be limited.

For Interactive Wildlife Sanctuaries

Introduction

Should animal sanctuaries and wildlife parks allow human interaction with species deemed harmless to humans?

Narrative

Animal sanctuaries are facilities where animals that have been abused or used in lab testing can go to live out their lives in a natural environment. They are not open to the public and do not engage in animal breeding. There are also wildlife parks. In wildlife parks, some interaction between people and animals is allowed (for example, petting rabbits). These two groups often criticize each other's goals. People who believe that humans should protect wildlife favor interaction. Those who believe that the rights of an individual animal should never be violated prefer to keep animals away from humans.

Writer's Position

There are several reasons why animal sanctuaries should allow human interaction.

Advantageous

First of all, interactive wildlife sanctuaries are advantageous. For science classes, wildlife parks provide a great opportunity for students to learn about species that are not native to their areas. For social studies classes, students can learn how animals have interacted with human beings for centuries by, for example, riding a dromedary camel and learning about the ancient caravans. At these parks, young people also develop affection for animals, which helps them to become good stewards of the earth as adults.

Necessary

Second, wildlife parks are necessary. For one thing, interaction is necessary so that the animals are more trusting of humans. This is important because when animals require medical attention, they need to trust people enough to allow the veterinarian to get close. In addition, wildlife parks assist in the breeding of endangered species. One such species is the tiger. Some cub tigers are now born and raised in several such facilities, including a wildlife park in Florida called Dade City's Wild Things. Kathy Stearnes, the founder, points out that if places like her park do not raise cubs, the world is not going to have any tigers left.[44]

Conclusion

In conclusion, interaction with animals is advantageous for education and necessary for the medical treatment and survival of species. Therefore, animal sanctuaries should allow interaction with humans.

EXERCISE 11.2: Analyzing Thesis

Directions: Examine the organization of the two Theses about animal sanctuaries and wildlife parks by answering the questions below.

1. Look over the first three paragraphs of each essay. Are they the same or different?

    a. The two Introductions are:

    • <u>the same.</u>

    • different.

b. The two Backgrounds are:

- <u>the same.</u>
- different.

c. The two statements of the Writer's Opinion are:

- the same.
- <u>different</u>.

2. Each essay uses two approaches to support the Writer's Opinion.

   a. What two approaches are used in the essay *against* animal interaction with humans?

   - Interaction is <u>*unjust*</u> to individual animals.
   - Non-interaction is <u>*necessary*</u> for rescued animals.

   b. What two approaches are used in the essay *for* animal interaction with humans?

   - Interaction is <u>*advantageous*</u> for education and stewardship.
   - Interaction is <u>*necessary*</u> for medical attention and breeding.

EXERCISE 11.3: Brainstorming Approaches to Thesis

Directions: Below are several topics suitable for a Thesis—some are proposals for the family and some are for the school. With a partner, decide which arguments would be the most persuasive: one for the proposal and one against it. The first one serves as an example.

Teacher's Edition

Approaches:

- **Necessary or unnecessary**—and why
- **Advantageous or disadvantageous**—and why
- **Legal or illegal**—and why
- **Customary or not customary**—and why

I. Topics for the Family

1. Should we install a swimming pool in our backyard?

    a. Yes, we should.

    Approach: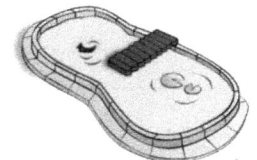

    Advantageous: good exercise

    b. No, we should not.

    Approach: *Unnecessary: other pools are available in the city*

2. Should our family establish a later bedtime during summertime?

    a. Yes, we should.

    Approach:

    _____

    b. No, we should not.

    Approach:

    _____

Thesis | 167

3. Should our family (add/drop/keep) cable TV? (Choose either *add*, *drop*, or *keep*.)

   a. Yes, we should.

      Approach:

      _____

   b. No, we should not.

      Approach:

      _____

II. Topics for Our School

4. Should our school offer Spanish classes?

   a. Yes, it should.

      Approach:

      _____

   b. No, it should not.

      Approach:

      _____

5. Should the sixth-graders be required to take a class trip to another (state / country)? (Choose either *state* or *country*.)

   a. Yes, it should.

      Approach:

      _____

b. No, it should not.

Approach: _____

EXERCISE 11.4: Converting Your Notes to an Essay

Directions: Choose one of the topics from Exercise 11.3 above and compose a paragraph that argues for or against the proposal. Be sure to follow the organization pattern presented in this chapter.

Teachers: This could be used as an individual assignment, an assignment with a partner, or a class-as-a-whole exercise, using the whiteboard.

Quills #1

Your teacher will give you the instructions you need to write a Thesis.

LAW

Chapter 12

Introduction

The Mark of the Beast
Revelation 13:16-18

The Bible's book of Revelation is classified as a book of prophecy. In Chapter 13, the apostle John foretold the rise of two beasts. Of the second beast, he wrote:

> [16]Also it causes all, both small and great, both rich and poor, both free and slave, to be marked on the right hand or the forehead, [17]so that no one can buy or sell unless he has the mark, that is, the name of the beast or the number of its name. [18]This calls for wisdom: let the one who has understanding calculate the number of the beast, for it is the number of a man, and his number is 666.

Here we have an example of a tyrannical law that has dire consequences for people. Imagine not being able to sell anything to make money, or, if you had money, not being able to buy anything with it—unless you had the tyrant's tattoo on your right hand or your forehead. People might become extremely upset about such a law—and, from the point of view of those who live in freedom, rightfully so.

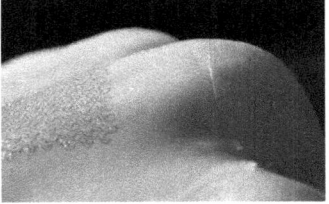

Electronic Tattoo

In ancient Greece, which was the birthplace of democracy, laws were not passed until every interested citizen had a right to express his views in the assembly—and, even then, it was not elected representatives, but the citizens themselves, who voted directly on the laws. For this reason, in Greek schools, Law arguments were considered the highest goal of the progymnasmata.

The purpose of this chapter is to familiarize you with the techniques of Law arguments and give you an opportunity to practice them.

Definition and Purpose

1. A Law argument is a composition or speech in which a person tries to persuade others to vote for or against a law.

2. The law under discussion could be a proposed law or a law already on the books. If the law is already on the books, people would be arguing for or against its repeal. That is, they would be arguing whether to keep or to get rid of the law.

Approaches to Law

This chapter introduces four approaches one can use when arguing for or against a law or rule. As with Thesis, you can think of approaches as reasons. For example you might ask if the law is:

- necessary or unnecessary?
- advantageous or disadvantageous?
- legal or illegal?
- just or unjust?

Teacher's Edition

The chart below explains the approaches and gives examples based on the tattoo issue raised in Revelation 13:16-18.

Necessary or Unnecessary?	Explain why it is or is not necessary to pass this law. Is there a problem that needs to be fixed? Or is there another way to solve the problem without a new law?
	**Example:** There are other ways to buy and sell. The tattoo is not needed.

Advantageous or Disadvantageous?	Explain why it would be helpful or harmful to pass the law. Would it help people, or just end up creating more problems?
	**Example:** Requiring such a tattoo would be very harmful to people of faith, who would refuse it for religious reasons. They would not even be able to buy food, clothing, or shelter.

Law | 173

Legal or Illegal?	Explain that this law does or does not conflict with any other law. Argue that the law is or is not Constitutional.
	Example: Freedom of religion is guaranteed by the Constitution. The government cannot force people to do something against their religion.

Fair or Unfair?	Explain how the proposal is fair to all people or unfair to some people.
	Example: The law requiring such a tattoo would discriminate against people of faith. It is unfair to treat one group differently from another.

IMPORTANT NOTE: As with Thesis, it is not necessary in Law to use all of the approaches in any one composition. The writer can pick and choose those approaches which are best for the topic at hand.

EXERCISE 12.1: Identifying Approaches to Law

Directions: Please begin by reading the introductory note about the call for a voting rights bill in 1965. Following the note are some excerpts from the speech of President Lyndon B. Johnson (1908-73). Work with a partner to determine which approach the President was using in each case.

Teacher's Edition

Lyndon Baines Johnson

Note: Approximately 100 years after the end of the Civil War, many African-Americans, especially in the Southern states, were being denied the opportunity to vote. Therefore, President Lyndon B. Johnson went before Congress on March 15, 1965, and urged the legislators to write and pass a voting rights bill. In the narrative portion of his speech, the President outlined some of the ways in which African-Americans were being denied their right to vote. He said, for example, "The Negro citizen may go to register only to be told that the day is wrong, or the hour is late, or the official in charge is absent. And if he persists, and if he manages to present himself to the registrar, he may be disqualified because he did not spell out his middle name or because he abbreviated a word on the application."[45] He then proceeded to lay out his reasons why a voting rights bill was needed. Some of these reasons appear below.

1. **Excerpt:** "Our fathers believed that if this noble view of the rights of man was to flourish, it must be rooted in democracy. The most basic right of all was the right to choose your own leaders. . . . Many of the issues of civil rights are very complex and most difficult. But about this there can and should be no argument. Every American citizen must have an equal right to vote. . . . Yet the harsh fact is that in many places in this country men and women are kept from voting simply because they are Negroes. . . . . In such a case our duty must be clear to all of us. The *Constitution* says that no person shall be kept from voting because of his race or his color. We have all sworn an oath before God to support and to defend that *Constitution*. We must now act in obedience to that oath."

   Question: The italicized words in this passage show that President Johnson thought that his proposal was certainly:

   A. <u>legal</u>.   B. advantageous.

3. **Excerpt:** "To those [in the South] who seek to avoid action by their National Government in their own communities; who want to and who seek to maintain purely local control over elections, the answer is simple:
   - Open your polling places to *all* your people.
   - Allow men and women to register and vote *whatever the color of their skin.*
   - Extend the rights of citizenship to *every citizen* of this land."

Question: The italicized words in the bulleted sentences show that in this passage Johnson was arguing that the laws governing voting should be:

   A. just (fair) for everyone.   B. advantageous for the economy.

3. **Excerpt:** "The time of justice has now come. I tell you that I believe sincerely that no force can hold it back. It is right in the eyes of man and God that it should come. And when it does, I think that day will *brighten the lives of every American*."

   Question: President Johnson here emphasized that passing the Civil Rights Bill would be:

   A. advantageous to all.   B. necessary for survival.

EXERCISE 12.2: Choosing Approaches to Support or Oppose a Law

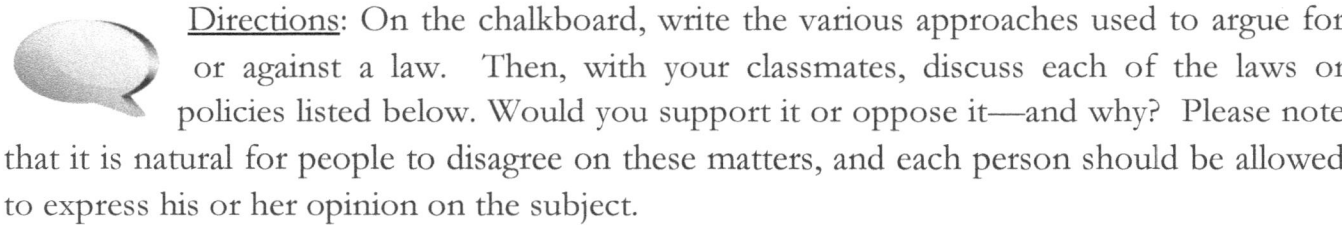

Directions: On the chalkboard, write the various approaches used to argue for or against a law. Then, with your classmates, discuss each of the laws or policies listed below. Would you support it or oppose it—and why? Please note that it is natural for people to disagree on these matters, and each person should be allowed to express his or her opinion on the subject.

Write on the board:

- Necessary or not unnecessary?
- Advantageous or disadvantageous?
- Legal or illegal?
- Just or unjust?

Discuss:

1. In Quincy, Massachusetts, people who live in public housing (residences owned by the government) are not allowed to smoke inside their residences. Is this a good law? Why or why not?

2. In Texas, in 2013 the state government passed a law which ensures students and teachers their right to use phrases like "Merry Christmas" and "Happy Hanukkah" in school. Is this a good law? Why or why not?

3. In 2012 in New York City, to improve the health of the citizens, Mayor Michael Bloomberg announced that 32-ounce soft drinks could no longer be sold. (However, it was still legal to buy two 16-ounce drinks.) Is this a good law? Why or why not?

4. A middle school in Pennsylvania banned students from wearing Ugg brand boots because students were hiding cell phones in them. Is this a good rule? Why or why not?

Organization

When writing for or against a law, follow this plan of organization:

1. **Introduction:** State the law (or proposed law) in a neutral tone. That is, do not tip your hand as to whether you support it or not.

2. **Narrative:** Without taking sides, explain why some people support the law and others oppose it.

3. **Writer's Opinion:** State whether you are for or against the law.

4. **Arguments:** Choose those approaches which are relevant to your position and develop each in standard "zigzag" style. Each one will have its own paragraph.

5. **Conclusion:** Briefly drive home your point.

Model Law Essays

Arguments *for* Licensing Bikers

Introduction

Should bicyclists be required to have a cycling license as drivers have to have a driver's license?

Narrative

Motorists often complain about the dangers posed by bicyclists sharing the streets. In 2012, 726 cyclists were killed in crashes with automobiles.[46] This number was up 6% from the previous year. Some authorities argue that educating and licensing bicyclists would make bike riding safer for everyone.

Writer's Position

There are two main reasons why bicyclists should be licensed.

Advantageous

First, educating and licensing bicyclists would be advantageous. It would help to reduce the number of accidents that result in death or serious injury. Before receiving a license, bicyclists would have to prove that they understood the laws of the road and knew what the law required of them in terms of signaling and stopping at lights. They could also learn the hazards of weaving in and out of traffic. All these measures would increase bike safety and save lives.

Just

Second, requiring cyclists to have licenses would be just. At the present time, it is unfair that automobile drivers have to take driver's education, take tests, and pay fees for licenses while cyclists get a free pass. The unfairness of the present system creates anger amongst drivers, which creates unpleasant incidents where drivers shout unkind things to cyclists. If both were required to have licenses, bicyclists and motorists would stop resenting each other.

Conclusion

In conclusion, since licensing cyclists would be advantageous and just, those who operate bicycles should be required to take lessons and pass tests to receive a license to ride on the city's streets.

Arguments *against* Licensing Bikers

Introduction

Should bicyclists be required to have a cycling license as drivers have to have a driver's license?

Background

Motorists often complain about the dangers posed by bicyclists sharing the streets. In 2012, 726 cyclists were killed in crashes with automobiles. This number was up 6% from the previous year. Some authorities argue that educating and licensing bicyclists would make bike riding safer for everyone.

Writer's Position

There are two main reasons why bicyclists should be not licensed.

Unnecessary

First, it is not necessary for bicyclists to be licensed. Police can and do already pull cyclists over if they commit a violation. Having a license would not make such a practice easier. Also, it is not necessary to collect money from cyclists to pay for road repairs because bicycles do not cause wear and tear on roads in the same way that cars, trucks, and busses do. In addition, cyclists are already paying taxes used for roads in other ways, such as sales tax.

Disadvantageous

Second, the process of licensing bicyclists has proved disadvantageous in cities which tried it. In the Canadian city of Ottawa, for example, authorities repealed the law in part because it created bad public relations between children and the police.[47]

Conclusion

In conclusion, since licensing is unnecessary and disadvantageous, those who operate bicycles should not be required to take lessons and pass tests to receive a license to ride on the city's streets

EXERCISE 12.3: Examining Law Arguments

 Directions: Examine the organization of the arguments for and against licensing bicyclists by answering the questions below.

1. Look over the first three paragraphs of each essay. Are they the same or different?

   a. The two Introductions are:
      - <u>the same.</u>
      - different.

   b. The two Backgrounds are:
      - <u>the same.</u>
      - different.

   c. The two statements of the Writer's Opinion are:
      - the same.
      - <u>different.</u>

2. Each essay uses two approaches to support the Writer's Opinion.

   a. What two approaches are used in the essay *for* licensing cyclists?
      - Licensing is *advantageous*.
      - Licensing is *just*.

   b. What two approaches are used in the essay *against* licensing cyclists??
      - Licensing is *unnecessary*.
      - Licensing is *disadvantageous*.

Teacher's Edition

EXERCISE 12.4: Brainstorming Approaches

 Directions: Below are topics suitable for Law arguments. With a partner, decide which approaches would be best to persuade an audience: one *for* the proposal and one *against* it. The first one serves as an example.

Approaches:

- **Necessary or unnecessary**—and why.
- **Advantageous or disadvantageous**—and why.
- **Legal or illegal**—and why.
- **Just or unjust**—and why.

1. Should school boards prohibit the use of dangerous animals as school mascots?

    a. Yes, they should.

    Approach:

    Advantageous because children will not start to think that dangerous animals are their friends.

    b. No, they should not.

    Approach:

    Unnecessary because there are other ways to teach children about dangerous animals.

2. Since some homes have unclean kitchens, should schools ban students from bringing homemade birthday cake or cookies to share with classmates?

    a. Yes.

    Approach:

    _____

    _____

Law | 181

b. No.

Approach:

_____

_____

3. Should schools allow candy and soda pop to be sold at lunchtime and before and after school?
   a. Yes.

   Approach:

   _____

   _____

   b. No.

   Approach:

   _____

   _____

EXERCISE 12:5: Converting Your Notes to a Paragraph

Directions: Choose one of the topics from Exercise 12.3 above and compose a paragraph that argues for or against the rule.

 **Quills #1**

Your teacher will give you the instructions you need to write a Law argument.

Teacher's Edition

Endnotes

1 George A. Kennedy, *Progymnasmata: Greek Textbooks of Prose Composition and Rhetoric*. Atlanta: Society of Biblical Literature, 2003. xi–xii.
2 Quintilian. *Institutes of Oratory*. Ed. Lee Honeycutt. Trans. John Selby Watson. Iowa State. 2006. Kindle file.
3 *The Fables of Aesop*. Trans. Joseph Jacobs. 1894. *Wikisource*. 11 Sept. 2012. Web. 8 May 2015.
4 *The Fables of Aesop*. Trans. Joseph Jacobs. 1894. *Wikisource*. 11 Sept. 2012. Web. 8 May 2015.
5 *Three Hundred Aesop's Fables*. Trans. George Fyler Townsend. 16 Apr. 2012. Web. 8 May 2015.
6 *Three Hundred Aesop's Fables*. Trans. George Fyler Townsend. 1867. 14 Apr. 2012. Web. 8 May 2012.
7 *Three Hundred Aesop's Fables*. Trans. George Fyler Townsend. 1867. 11 Sept. 2012. Web. 8 May 2012.
8 "Washington during the War." *Macmillan's Magazine*. 1862. 6:24. Web. 2 Sept. 2014.
9 "Speech of Frederick Douglass at the Third Decade Celebration of the Anti-Slavery Society in Philadelphia." *Pacific Appeal* [San Francisco]. 31 Feb. 1864. 1. *California Digital Newspaper Collection*. Web. 2 Sept. 2014.
10 The text is a paraphrase of Suetonius' description in "The Personal Traits of Julius Caesar." *Readings in Ancient History: Rome and the West*. Ed. William Stearns Davis. 2:159. Boston: Allyn, 1913.
11 *The Evening World* [New York]). 18 Feb. 1922. 7. Final extra edition. Web. 3 Sept. 2014.
12 The examples in this section are taken from *Plutarch's Lives*, Vol. 1.
13 "Pecos Bill." *VOA Learning English*. Voice of America. 28 Nov 2009. Web. 20 Aug 2014.
14 Charles E. Brown. "Paul Bunyan." *Paul Bunyan Tales*. 2nd ed. Madison: U of Wisconsin P, 1927. 5. *Hathi Trust*. n.d., Web. 20 Aug 2014.
15 The examples in this section are from *Davy Crockett's Riproarious Shemales and Sentimental Sisters: Women's Tall Tales from the Crockett Almanacs (1835-1856)*. Ed. Michael A. Lofaro. Mechanicsburg, PA: Stackpole, 2001.
16 Charles E. Brown. 4.
17 Addison Erwin Sheldon. *History and Stories of Nebraska*. Lincoln: University P, 1913.
18 George Armstrong Custer. *My Life on the Plains*. New York: Sheldon, 1874. *Internet Archive*. 2009. Web. 22 Aug 2014.
19 W. Aldis Wright, ed. *Generydes: A Romance in Seven-Line Stanzas*. London: Trübner, 1878. 144.
20 Wayne Whipple. *The Story of Young Abraham Lincoln*. Philadelphia: Altemus, 1918.
21 "Anecdote." *Merriam-Webster.com*. 2015. Web. 3 Dec. 2014.
22 Sophocles. *The Antigone of Sophocles in Greek and English*. Trans. R. C. Jebb. Boston: Ginn, 1894. *Internet Archive*. 2001. Web. 25 Sept. 2014.
23 Thomas Jamescia. "Peewee Football Team Creates Appreciation Day for Bullied Boy." *ABC News*. 25 Nov. 2013. Web. 25 Sept. 2014.
24 David R. Barnhart. "Corrie ten Boom: Love in Action." *The Vine and the Branches*. 29.3 (2014): n.pag. Abiding Word Ministries. Web. 27 Jan. 2015.
25 "Mother Teresa of Calcutta: Peacemaker, Pioneer, Legend." Eternal World Television Network. 19 Oct. 2003. Web. 27 Jan. 2015.
26 Dwight D. Eisenhower. "Eulogy for Sir Winston Churchill." *In Tribute: Eulogies of Famous People*. Ed. Ted Tobias. Lanham MD: Scarecrow, 1999. 18-20.
27 Harold A. Shaitberger, et al. "Raw Data: Firefighters Union Letter on Rudy Giuliani." *FoxNews.com*. 8 Mar 2007. Web. 27 Jan 2015.
28 "Woolsey Lambastes Ames as Worse than Benedict Arnold." *AP News Archive*. 19 Jul 1994. Web. 27 Jan 2015.
29 Traci Peterson. "Charles 'The Old Roman' Comiskey." *Famous American Trials: The Black Sox Trial, 1921*. University of Missouri at Kansas City. n.d. Web. 29 Jan. 2015.
30 Paul Franklin Baum. "Riddle 17." *Anglo-Saxon Riddles of the* Exeter Book. Durham Duke UP, 1963. *Wikisource*. 13 Aug 2014. Web. 19 Nov. 2014. Creative Commons Attribution-ShareAlike License. <http://creativecommons.org/licenses/by-sa/3.0/> [The word *mortals* was changed to *people*.]
31 Billy Graham. *Hope for Each Day: Words of Wisdom and Faith*. Nashville: Thomas Nelson, 2008. 22.
32 William Shakespeare. *King Lear*. I.4.285-86. Shakespeare Online. n.d. Web. 29 Apr. 2015.
33 "Scorn." *Merriam-Webster.com*. 2015. Web. 29 Apr. 2015.
34 Brothers Grimm. "Little Red-Cap." *Grimm's Household Tales*. Vol. 1. Trans. Margaret Hunt. London: Bell, 1884. *Wikisource*. Creative Commons Attribution Share-Alike License. < http://creativecommons.org/licenses/by-sa/3.0/>. 29 Jun 2011. Web. 1 May 2015.
35 Mike Everhart. "Something about Plesiosaurs (Elasmosaurs)." *Oceans of Kansas*. 9 May 2012. Web. 13 Apr 2015.
36 A. E. Housman. Poem XL. *A Shropshire Lad*. Public Domain Poetry. n.d. Web.19 May 2015.
37 Christina Rossetti. "Good Friday." *Public Domain Poetry*. n.d. Web. 19 May 2015.
38 Henry Wadsworth Longfellow. *Evangeline: A Tale of Arcadie*. Public Domain Poetry. n.d. Web.19 May 2015.
39 William Blake. "The Little Black Boy." *Public Domain Poetry*. n.d. Web.19 May 2015.
40 "The Horse and the Stag." Trans. George Fyler Townsend. 1887. *Wikisource*. Creative Commons Attribution share-Alike License. <http://creativecommons.org/licenses/by-sa/3.0/>.
41 Theodore Roosevelt. "What We Can Expect of the American Boy." *St. Nicholas Magazine*. May 1900. 27.571-74. Print.
42 Rachel Hartigan Shea. "Are Wildlife Sanctuaries Good for Animals?" *National Geographic.com* 20 Mar. 2014. Web. 1 Apr. 2015. <http://news.nationalgeographic.com/news/2014/03/140320-animal-sanctuary-wildlife-exotic-tiger-zoo/>.
43 "Mocha's Story: Living Lawnmower, Went on the Roof." *Harvest Home Sanctuary*. 18 Sept. 2013. Web. 1 Apr. 2015. <http://harvesthomesanctuary.org/animals/mocha/>.

44 Shea.

45 All quotes in this exercise are from "President Lyndon B. Johnson's Special Message to Congress: The American Promise, March 16, 1965." LBJ Presidential Library. University of Texas. 6 June 2007. Web. 10 June 2015. <http://www.lbjlib.utexas.edu/johnson/archives.hom/speeches.hom/650315.asp>.

46 National Highway Traffic Safety Administration. U.S. Department of Transportation. Apr. 2014. Web. 3 Apr. 2015. <http://www-nrd.nhtsa.dot.gov/Pubs/812018.pdf>.

47 "Why Aren't Cyclists Licensed?" *Bike Calgary*. n.d. Web. 3 Apr. 2015. <www.bikecalgary.org/licensing>.

Image Attribution

Images available through licensure are listed below.

Cover

"Fox Writing with a Quill." Will. *A Journey round My Skull*. *Flickr*. 31 Mar. 2010. Web. 28 July 2015. <https://www.flickr.com/photos/ajourneyroundmyskull/>. Creative Commons Attribution 2.0 Generic. <https://creativecommons.org/licenses/by/2.0>.

Chapter 1, "Fable"

"The Lion and the Mouse." Hutchinson Page. Creative Commons Attribution Share-Alike 3.0 License. <http://creativecommons.org/licenses/by-sa/3.0/>. *Wikispaces*. < http://hutchinson-page.wikispaces.com/What+is+a+FABLE%3F>.

"Wolf and Crane." Laura K. Gibbs. *Flikr*. <https://www.flickr.com/photos/38299630@N05/3679519425>. Creative Commons Attribution 2.0 Generic. <https://creativecommons.org/licenses/by/2.0>.

"The Serpent and the Eagle." n.d. Web. 8 May 2015. <http://widgets.bestmoodle.net/Scriptdata/AesopEngPoetry.html>.

"John Everett Millais - Parable of the Unjust Judge [Persistent Widow]." John Everett Millais. <http://myweb.tiscali.co.uk/speel/pici/millais3.jpg>. Licensed under Public Domain via Wikimedia Commons. <http://commons.wikimedia.org/wiki/File:John_Everett_Millais_-_Parable_of_the_Unjust_Judge.jpg#/media/File:John_Everett_Millais_-_Parable_of_the_Unjust_Judge.jpg>.

Chapter 2, "Description"

"Julius Caesar." *Wikispaces Classroom*. 2105. Web. 13 August 2015. <http://ravenseniors.wikispaces.com/Julius+Caesar+period+4>.

"Jim Thorpe Canton Bulldogs 1915-20." Unattributed. Heritage Auctions. Licensed under Public Domain via *Wikimedia Commons*. <http://commons.wikimedia.org/wiki/File:Jim_Thorpe_Canton_Bulldogs_1915-20.png#/media/File:Jim_Thorpe_Canton_Bulldogs_1915-20.png>.

"Theseus Crommyonian Sow Louvre G637." English: Sotades Painter or Hippacontist Painter (Beazley). User:Bibi Saint-Pol. Own work. 2007-07-21. <http://commons.wikimedia.org/wiki/File:Theseus_Crommyonian_Sow_Louvre_G637.jpg#/media/File:Theseus_Crommyonian_Sow_Louvre_G637.jpg>. Licensed under Public Domain via *Wikimedia Commons*. 22 July 2007. Web. 11 May 2015.

"Chambers 1908 Sloop." Rev. Thomas Davidson 1856-1923 (ed.). *Chambers's Twentieth Century Dictionary of the English Language*. <http://commons.wikimedia.org/wiki/File:Chambers_1908_Sloop.png#/media/File:Chambers_1908_Sloop.png>. Licensed under Public Domain via *Wikimedia Commons*.

"Wood Axe." Brittgow. *Flickr*. Creative Commons Attribution 2.0 Generic. <https://creativecommons.org/licenses/by/2.0>. <https://www.flickr.com/photos/brittgow/4781607809>.

Chapter 3, "Narrative"

"Philippe de Champaigne - Moses with the Ten Commandments - WGA04717." Philippe de Champaigne. Web Gallery of Art: Image Info about artwork. Licensed under Public Domain via *Wikimedia Commons*. <http://commons.wikimedia.org/wiki/File:Philippe_de_Champaigne_-_Moses_with_the_Ten_Commandments_-_WGA04717.jpg#/media/File:Philippe_de_Champaigne_-_Moses_with_the_Ten_Commandments_-_WGA04717.jpg>.

"Prefecture map of Crete (Greece)." SilentResident,Philly boy92. <http://commons.wikimedia.org/wiki/File:Precture map of Crete (Greece).svg#/ media/File:Prefecture_map_of_Crete_(Greece).svg>. Own work. Licensed under CC BY-SA 3.0 via *Wikimedia Commons*. <http://creativecommons.org/licenses/by-sa/3.0/deed.en>.

Teacher's Edition

"'The Fall of Icarus,' 17th century, Musée Antoine Vivenel." Wmpearl. Own work. Licensed under Public Domain via *Wikimedia Commons*
<http://commons.wikimedia.org/wiki/File:%27The_Fall_of_Icarus%27,_17th_century,_Mus%C3%A9e_Antoine_Vivenel.JPG#/media/File:%27The_Fall_of_Icarus%27,_17th_century,_Mus%C3%A9e_Antoine_Vivenel.JPG>.

"Pecos Bill Lassos a Tornado." Maroonbeard. Own work. <http://commons.wikimedia.org/wiki/File:Pecos_Bill_Lassos_A_Tornado.jpg#/media/File:Pecos_Bill_Lassos_A_Tornado.jpg>. Licensed under CC BY-SA 3.0 via *Wikimedia Commons*. <http://creativecommons.org/licenses/by-sa/3.0/deed.en>.

"Baldknobbers". <http://en.wikipedia.org/wiki/File:Baldknobbersrr.jpg#/media/File:Baldknobbersrr.jpg>. Licensed under PD-US via *Wikipedia*. 9 May 2006. Web. 11 May 2015.

"Teacher Asking Question." Rodney Tan Chai Whatt. *English Teachers' Network*. n.d. Web. 11 May 2015.
<http://englishteachernet.blogspot.com/2011/02/story-with-moral-10-easy-questions-or-1.html>.

"U. S. Cavalry Soldiers during the Battle of Beecher Island." Anonymous. *Harper's New Monthly Magazine*. June 1895. 57. File copied from http://digital.denverlibrary.org/u?/p15330coll22,38419. Licensed under Public Domain via *Wikimedia Commons*. <http://commons.wikimedia.org/wiki/File:U._S._Cavalry_soldiers_during_the_Battle_of_Beecher_Island.jpg#/media/File:U._S._Cavalry_soldiers_during_the_Battle_of_Beecher_Island.jpg>.

Chapter 4, "Writing a Good Paragraph"

"1-albero, Taccuino Sanitatis, Casanatense 4182." Unknown master - book scan. Licensed under Public Domain via *Wikimedia Commons*.< http://commons.wikimedia.org/wiki/File:1-albero,_Taccuino_Sanitatis,_Casanatense_4182..jpg#/media/File:1-albero,_Taccuino_Sanitatis,_Casanatense_4182..jpg>.

"Citra Coca Cola" by Source. Licensed under Fair use via *Wikipedia*.
<http://en.wikipedia.org/wiki/File:Citra_Coca_Cola.png#/media/File:Citra_Coca_Cola.png>.

"Coca-Cola Orange" by Source. Licensed under Fair use via *Wikipedia*. <http://en.wikipedia.org/wiki/File:Coca-Cola_Orange.jpg#/media/File:Coca-Cola_Orange.jpg>.

"Coke Blak bottle" by Source. Licensed under Fair use via *Wikipedia*.
<http://en.wikipedia.org/wiki/File:Coke_Blak_bottle.png#/media/File:Coke_Blak_bottle.png>.

"Krakatoa Erupting 1883." *Wikispaces Classroom*. Creative Commons Attribution Share-Alike 3.0 License.
<http://volcanoes6.wikispaces.com/krakatoa>.

"His Master's Voice." Licensed under Public Domain via *Wikimedia Commons*.
<http://commons.wikimedia.org/wiki/File:His_Master%27s_Voice.jpg#/media/File:His_Master%27s_Voice.jpg>.

"Brain-Controlled Prosthetic Arm 2." FDA.< https://flic.kr/p/9gFr4x>. Licensed under Public Domain via *Wikimedia Commons*. <http://commons.wikimedia.org/wiki/File:Brain-Controlled_Prosthetic_Arm_2.jpg#/media/File:Brain-Controlled_Prosthetic_Arm_2.jpg>. 5 Aug. 2014.Web. 11 May 2015.

Chapter 5, "Proverb and Chreia"

"Chess Pieces." Aaron W. *YouMagine.*. 4 Feb 2015. Web. 7 May 2015. <https://www.youmagine.com/designs/chess-pieces.pdf>. Creative Commons Attribution Share-Alike License. < http://creativecommons.org/licenses/by-sa/3.0/deed.en_US>.

"Sejanus Tiberius As." Classical Numismatic Group, Inc. <http://www.cngcoins.com>.
http://commons.wikimedia.org/wiki/File:Sejanus_Tiberius_As.jpg#/media/File:Sejanus_Tiberius_As.jpg>. Licensed under CC BY-SA 3.0 via *Wikimedia Commons*. <http://creativecommons.org/licenses/by-sa/3.0/deed.en>.

"A Christmas Carol: Ignorance and Want." Public domain. *Wikimedia Commons*.
<http://commons.wikimedia.org/wiki/File:A_Christmas_Carol_-_Ignorance_and_Want.jpg>.

"Plato and Aristotle." *Wikispaces Classroom*. <http://ast-philosophy.wikispaces.com/Sergio+and+Sergio>.

"Benjamin Franklin." *Wikispaces Classroom*. <http://reinsteinrevolutionper2.wikispaces.com/Treaty+of+Paris>.

"Young Lincoln by Charles Keck." Sculpture: Charles Keck (1875-1951). Photograph: Work of uploader: Alanscottwalker (talk) 11:21, 12 October 2010 (UTC). Own work. Licensed under Public Domain via *Wikimedia Commons*.
<http://commons.wikimedia.org/wiki/File:Young_Lincoln_By_Charles_Keck.JPG#/media/File:Young_Lincoln_By_Charles_Keck.JPG>.

"Six Hats 1 by kattekrab." *Open Clip Art*. <https://openclipart.org/detail/15892/six-hats-1>.

Chapter 6, "Encomium and Invective"

"Drawing of Ancient Pergamon." Anonymous. <https://en.wikipedia.org/wiki/File:Drawing_of_ancient_Pergamon.jpg. Licensed under Public Domain via *Wikimedia Commons* - http://commons.wikimedia.org/wiki/File:Drawing_of_ancient_Pergamon.jpg#/media/File:Drawing_of_ancient_Pergamon.jpg>.

"Star of David." *Wikispaces Classroom*. <http://mbalter.wikispaces.com/Star+of+David>.

"MotherTeresa 094" by © 1986 Túrelio (via Wikimedia-Commons), 1986 /. Licensed under CC BY-SA 2.0 de via *Wikimedia Commons*. <https://creativecommons.org/licenses/by/2.0/>. <http://commons.wikimedia.org/wiki/File:MotherTeresa_094.jpg#/media/File:MotherTeresa_094.jpg>.

"Winston Churchill." *Wikispaces Classroom.* <http://worldhistory2012emtcmh.wikispaces.com/The+Cold+War>.

"Frontspiece of *A Blind Girl*." Public Domain. <http://en.wikipedia.org/wiki/File:A_Blind_Girl.jpg>.

"September 14 2001 Ground Zero 03." U.S. Navy photo by Photographer's Mate 2nd Class Jim Watson. (RELEASED) U.S. Navy photo http://www.navy.mil/view_image.asp?id=2490. Licensed under Public Domain via *Wikimedia Commons*. <http://commons.wikimedia.org/wiki/File:September_14_2001_Ground_Zero_03.jpg#/media/File:September_14_2001_Ground_Zero_03.jpg>.

"Aldrich Ames Mugshot." Staff. Federal Bureau of Investigation. Federal Bureau of Investigation. Licensed under Public Domain via *Wikimedia Commons*. <http://commons.wikimedia.org/wiki/File:Aldrich_Ames_mugshot.jpg#/media/File:Aldrich_Ames_mugshot.jpg>.

"Charles Comiskey." Anonymous. < http://www.archive.org/details/notablemenofchi00chic > Page 62. Licensed under Public Domain via *Wikimedia Commons*. http://commons.wikimedia.org/wiki/File:Charles_Comiskey.jpg#/media/File:Charles_Comiskey.jpg>.

"Death of Saul." Gustav Doré. Public Domain. <http://www.wikiart.org/en/gustave-dore/the-death-of-saul>.

Chapter 7, "Refutation and Confirmation"

"Le avventure di Pinocchio-pag107." Carlo Chiostri. File:Le avventure di Pinocchio.djvu. Licensed under Public Domain via *Wikimedia Commons*. < http://commons.wikimedia.org/wiki/File:Le_avventure_di_Pinocchio-pag107.jpg#/media/File:Le_avventure_di_Pinocchio-pag107.jpg>.

"The Riddle Book." <http://www.merrycoz.org/books/riddle/RIDDLE.HTM>.

"Brutus of Troy." Published by Guillaume Rouille (1518?-1589). "Promptuarii Iconum Insigniorum." Licensed under Public Domain via *Wikimedia Commons*. 30 Nov. 2009. Web. 17 June 2015. <https://commons.wikimedia.org/wiki/File:Brutus_of_troy.jpg#/media/File:Brutus_of_troy.jpg>.

"Dickens Gurney head." Jeremiah Gurney. Heritage Auction Gallery. Licensed under Public Domain via *Wikimedia Commons*. <http://commons.wikimedia.org/wiki/File:Dickens_Gurney_head.jpg#/media/File:Dickens_Gurney_head.jpg>.

"Mr Brownlow at the Bookstall." George Cruikshank - Oliver Twist. Licensed under Public Domain via *Wikimedia Commons*. <http://commons.wikimedia.org/wiki/File:Mr_Brownlow_at_the_bookstall.jpg#/media/File:Mr_Brownlow_at_the_bookstall.jpg>.

Chapter 8, "Commonplace"

"Fresques de la Passion du Christ de la chapelle Notre-Dame-des-Fontaines." *Wikimedia Commons*. <http://commons.wikimedia.org/wiki/File:La_Brigue_-_Chapelle_Notre-Dame-des-Fontaines_-_Nef_-_Fresques_de_la_Passion_du_Christ_-7.JPG>. Creative Commons Attribution/Share-Alike License. <http://creativecommons.org/licenses/by-sa/3.0/deed.en>.

"Goofus and Gallant: Don't Be That Guy." Ron Mader. *Flickr*. Creative Commons Share-Alike License 2.0 Generic. <https://creativecommons.org/licenses/by/2.0/>. 23 Aug. 2012. Web. 30 July 2015. <https://www.flickr.com/photos/planeta/7843884124>.

Chapter 9, "Comparison"

"Little Red Riding Hood." Walter Crane. Public domain. *Wikimedia Commons*. <http://commons.wikimedia.org/wiki/File:Walter_Crane26.jpg>..

"The House Built upon the Sand." *Old Books.* Public domain. <http://www.fromoldbooks.org/DJD-BiblePictures-NewTestament/pages/017-house-built-on-sand>.

"Mark Twain by AF Bradley." A.F. Bradley, New York - steamboattimes.com. Disponible bajo la licencia Dominio público vía *Wikimedia Commons*. <http://commons.wikimedia.org/wiki/File:Mark_Twain_by_AF_Bradley.jpg#/media/File:Mark_Twain_by_AF_Bradley.jpg>.

"Robert Louis Stevenson." Alberto - Ana Quiroga. Licensed under Public Domain via *Wikimedia Commons*. <http://commons.wikimedia.org/wiki/File:Robert-louis-stevenson.jpg#/media/File:Robert-louis-stevenson.jpg>.

"Hoaxed photo of the Loch Ness Monster." Source. Licensed under Fair use via *Wikipedia*. <http://en.wikipedia.org/wiki/File:Hoaxed_photo_of_the_Loch_Ness_monster.jpg#/media/File:Hoaxed_photo_of_the_Loch_Ness_monster.jpg>.

"Plesiosaur on Land." Heinrich Harder (1858-1935). <http://www.copyrightexpired.com/Heinrich_Harder/

plesiosaur_aquarium.html>. Licensed under Public Domain via *Wikimedia Commons*.
<http://commons.wikimedia.org/wiki/File:Plesiosaur_on_land.jpg#/media/File:Plesiosaur_on_land.jpg>.

Chapter 10, "Speech-in-Character"

"Alfred Edward Housman." E. O. Hoppe.<http://images.google.com/hosted/life/fd76be65c0baead9.html.>. Licensed under PD-US via *Wikipedia*. <http://en.wikipedia.org/wiki/File:Alfred_Edward_Housman.jpeg#/media/File:Alfred_Edward_Housman.jpeg>.

"John Bunyan." Licensed under Public Domain via *Wikimedia Commons*.
<http://commons.wikimedia.org/wiki/File:John_Bunyan.jpg#/media/File:John_Bunyan.jpg>.

"Sad and Doleful." *Pilgrim's Progress* by John Bunyan. Philadelphia: Altemus, 1890. Public Domain. *Wikimedia Commons*.
<http://commons.wikimedia.org/wiki/File:PProg_50_p115_SadAndDoleful.jpg>.

"Christina Rosetti." Christina Rossetti 3 by user:Phrood - based on [1]. Licensed under Public Domain via *Wikimedia Commons*.
<http://commons.wikimedia.org/wiki/File:Christina_Rossetti_3.jpg#/media/File:Christina_Rossetti_3.jpg>.

"Statue of Evangeline (Emmeline Labiche) in St. Martinville, Louisiana." Public Domain. *Wikimedia Commons*. 20 Jan. 2007. Web. 19 May 2015. <http://commons.wikimedia.org/wiki/File:Evangeline_statue_St_Martinville_Louisiana_closeup_trim.jpg>.

"Life of William Blake (1880), volume 1, frontispiece" by Schiavonetti, Phillips. *Gilchrist's Life*, 1880. Licensed under Public Domain via *Wikimedia Commons*.
<http://commons.wikimedia.org/wiki/File:Life_of_William_Blake_(1880),_volume_1,_frontispiece.png#/media/File:Life_of_William_Blake_(1880),_volume_1,_frontispiece.png>.

"How Should I Your True Love Know." *Old Book Art*. Public Domain. 19 May 2015.
<http://www.gallery.oldbookart.com/main.php?g2_itemId=15380 >.

"The Glass Mountain." *Old Book Art*. Public Domain. 19 May 2015.
<http://www.gallery.oldbookart.com/main.php?g2_itemId=15469>.

"Seven Ravens." *Old Book Art*. Public Domain. 19 May 2015.
<http://www.gallery.oldbookart.com/main.php?g2_itemId=15849>."There Sat a Man in an Iron Cage." *Pilgrim's Progress* by John Bunyan. Philadelphia: Altemus, 1890. Public Domain. *Wikimedia Commons*.
<http://commons.wikimedia.org/wiki/File:PProg_15_p45_ThereSatAManInAnIronCage.jpg>.

Chapter 11, "Thesis"

"The Stag and the Horse." Wenceslas Hollar. Public domain. *Wikimedia Commons*. 15 Mar. 2009. Web. 12 May 2015.
<https://commons.wikimedia.org/wiki/File:Wenceslas_Hollar_-_The_stag_and_the_horse_3.jpg>.

"Orator." "Communication in Ancient Rome." *Wikispaces Classroom*. 2006. Web. 12 May 2015. <https://ccit300-f06.wikispaces.com/Communication+in+ancient+Rome>. Creative Commons Attribution Share-Alike 2.5.
<http://creativecommons.org/licenses/by-sa/2.5/ License.

"Theodore Roosevelt." *Wikispaces Classroom*. <http://psontheimer.wikispaces.com/Mod+2+American+History>.

"Huckleberry Finn Book Cover." Boston Public Library. *Flikr*. <https://www.flickr.com/photos/boston_public_library/4404529592>. Creative Commons Attribution 2.0 Generic.
<https://creativecommons.org/licenses/by/2.0/>.

Chapter 12, "Law"

"Electronic Tattoo." "'Game-changing' Printed Tattoos May Replace Hefty Medical Monitors." *The Conversation*. 11 Aug. 2011. Web. 13 Aug. 2015. <http://theconversation.com/game-changing-printed-tattoos-may-replace-hefty-medical-monitors-2811>. Creative Commons Attribution –No Derivatives 4.0 International License. <http://creativecommons.org/licenses/by-nd/4.0/>.

"Official Presidential Portrait of President Lyndon Baines Johnson." Elizabeth Shoumatoff. 1968. Public Domain. *Wikimedia Commons*.
<http://commons.wikimedia.org/wiki/File:Ljohnson.jpeg>.

"Great Seal of the United States (reverse)." Ipankonin. This vector image was created with Inkscape. Own work. Licensed under CC BY-SA 3.0 via *Wikimedia Commons*. 25 Jan. 2008. Web. 10 June 2015. <http://commons.wikimedia.org/wiki/File:Great_Seal_of_the_United_States_(reverse).svg#/media/File:Great_Seal_of_the_United_States_(reverse).svg>.

www.ingramcontent.com/pod-product-compliance
Lightning Source LLC
Chambersburg PA
CBHW050748100426
42744CB00012BA/1932